Short Bike Rides™ Series

Short Bike Rides™ in Vermont

By
Sandy Duling

An East Woods Book

Old Saybrook, Connecticut

Copyright © 1997 by Sandra C. Duling

Short Bike Rides is a trademark of The Globe Pequot Press
Cover photograph © 1996 PhotoDisc, Inc.

Library of Congress Cataloging-in-Publication Data

Duling Sandy.
  Short bike rides in Vermont / Sandy Duling.—1st ed.
      p.   cm. — (Short bike rides series)
  "An East Woods book."
  Includes index
  ISBN 0-7627-0045-9
  1. Bicycle touring—Vermont—Guidebooks. 2. Vermont— Guidebooks.
I. Title. II. Series
  GV1045.5.V5D85   1997
  796.6'4'09743—dc21   96-54274
                                                        CIP

Acknowledgments

Thanks to all the friends who made trip suggestions, pedaled with me, patiently posed for photographs, provided bed and breakfast, and enthusiastically joined in the fun of this project: Mary Hamilton, Ann Foley, Pat Max, Joe Lauricella, Suzanne Gallagher, Peter Spitzform, Debbie Bethel, Helen Mango, Bob Smith, Fred Michel, Mike Hurley, and all the folks I've met along the way. Don Blades, darkroom technician, deserves particular credit for making the most of the film I sent him.

Without my family's help and encouragement, this book couldn't have been completed. Special thanks to Ennis Duling for photography, photography advice, and endless editing/proofreading. Andy Duling for being a patient companion, and Alec Duling for editing, lots of pedaling, and programming the elevation profiles, a most valuable addition to the book.

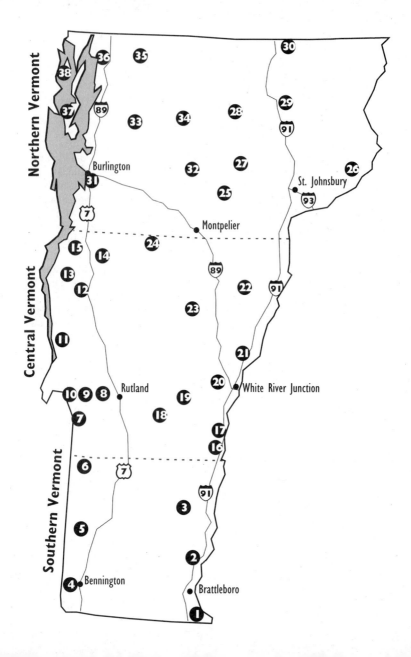

Contents

Introduction

Welcome to Vermont

According to the 1990 census, Vermont is the most rural of the fifty states (in other words, that among the states, Vermont has the greatest percentage of people living in rural areas). From a biker's point of view, that means lots of back roads with relatively sparse traffic. Add a wonderful variety of scenery, terrain that varies from flat to mountainous, historic sites, swimming holes, friendly general stores, and a population staunchly committed to an environmental ethic, and you've got the setting for wonderful biking.

Working on this book was a real pleasure. I knew it would be fun, but it was even more rewarding than I anticipated. My passion for biking has taken me, over the years, to many parts of Vermont; but here was an excuse to test ride new routes in all corners of the state. If, from the experience of these rides, I were to draw a single conclusion about my home state, it would be this: The beauty and variety of Vermont's scenery is surpassed only by the energy and individuality of its people. From the young man in Hartland who had just pedaled from San Francisco to the very spry 70-year-old woman at Lake Bomoseen who was out for a 20-mile jaunt, Vermont's bikers all seem to embody the hard-to-define qualities of the true Vermonter–a quirky individuality, tough-mindedness, concern for the environment, and a sense of adventure. And just as memorable are the nonbikers I met in my travels–who may, in fact, be bikers, but whom I happened to meet in other capacities: the keepers of general stores, who patiently dish out ice cream, directions, and local news; town clerks, who know the name of every road, path, and pothole; state park employees and volunteers; truck drivers; tractor and hay wagon drivers; librarians; fishermen; kids on playgrounds; town road crews. They've all waved, moved over, pondered directions, or lent a hand. It's my hope that readers of this collection of rides will have as much fun enjoying Vermont's scenery and people as I've had.

About the Rides

The rides included in this collection range from about 10 to about 30 miles. They were selected with the casual weekend cyclist in mind. Serious athletes interested in more strenuous rides can best use the book by putting two or more rides together, or by using the rides as starting points for longer excursions. You'll note on the outline map that the rides cluster along the edges of the state. The Green Mountains form a rugged north-south spine down the center of Vermont. A number of possible loops in the central part of the state were rejected because they cover quite difficult terrain, and because they were longer than the scope of this collection. The eastern and especially the western portions of the state, while certainly not flat, tend more toward rolling hills and farmland, and that's where you'll find the majority of these short trips. As well as length and difficulty of terrain, criteria used in selecting the rides included traffic, road surface, and presence of road shoulders. Sadly, I had to exclude a number of otherwise lovely rides because of volume of traffic or inadequacy of road shoulders. Other criteria were scenery and points of interest. Just about every ride has an interesting stop or two. Some have many such stops.

Directions, turns, and points of interest are indicated by mileage from the beginning of the ride. Mileages aim for accuracy to the tenth of a mile. Although the maps and directions will be good guides for anyone, the mileage indicators will be most useful for riders who have a "cyclocomputer" or some other type of odometer. Cyclocomputers are now quite inexpensive–less than twenty dollars for one with lots of fancy functions–and they are available from almost any bike shop or mail order supplier. Note that maps throughout the book are not of a uniform scale, and cannot really be used for comparisons. The little graphs included with each ride are "elevation profiles." While not designed to indicate precise elevation, or to depict every hill you'll encounter, they *are* produced on a uniform scale and should provide a useful general outline of the terrain each ride will cover.

Also included at the beginning of each ride is a (very) approximate pedaling time, an indication of places to stop for food, a quick list of points of interest, and a mention of bathroom facilities, if any are available. Most rides pass a general store or two, where sodas and snacks are available. General stores, however, typically do not have public rest rooms. Most of these rides are in very rural areas, where the "green door" rest room is the best bet.

Road signage in Vermont is inconsistent. Some towns name and mark even the tiniest roads. Other towns seem to adhere to the philosophy that everybody who needs to get around town probably knows where they're going, and road signs are something of a frill. You'll notice that directions sometimes indicate a turn onto a named road, sometimes simply onto a "hard-surface road to the right." In towns where signs are scarce, it's especially important to pay attention to mileages!

Safety

Wear a helmet. Most people who do a significant amount of biking will, eventually, take a tumble. Mine occurred while working on this book. My helmet broke, dispersing the blow, and I walked away from the accident. Without the helmet, what was a very minor accident would have resulted in a head injury. The helmets now available are designed to be lightweight and have good ventilation. Granted, they still look a little strange, but they work.

Ride single file and stay to the right. A surprising number of visiting cyclists are so delighted with the rural nature of Vermont's roads that they assume there is no traffic at all. They're sometimes found riding two or even three abreast down the center of the road. There will be traffic–often going both ways. Remember that what looks like a quaint country road to the visitor is, in fact, the main route between towns, to work, or to the big city for local folks.

Be sure your bike is in good working order. Check brakes, cables, and tires regularly.

Carry water and at least a small snack. Biking can be strenuous exercise, and especially in the summer, it doesn't take long to become dehydrated. Clear and pristine as Vermont's streams may appear, do not drink water from them without first treating it.

Be visible. The yellow biking jerseys people wear are more than a fashion statement–they're safer than duller colored shirts. Don't set out until daylight in the morning and stop riding before dusk. Be predictable; signal your intentions before turning. And watch especially carefully for cars backing out of parking areas.

Equipment

All rides in this collection are well suited to touring or road bikes. Most, in fact, were happily test ridden on a veritable antique of a French ten-speed. A few rides travel on short sections of dirt road, but none that aren't suitable for even the skinniest tires. Hybrid bikes (best described as a cross between a road bike and a mountain bike) seem to be the best sellers at present. Their wide range of gears and slightly wider tires make them a fine choice for most Vermont trips.

Other than bike and helmet, little additional equipment is absolutely necessary. A few simple tools for repair are a good idea: a mini pump, a tire patch kit, a spare tube, a couple of tire irons. Without these, a flat could mean a long walk. The possible need for extra clothing should always be considered. Vermont's weather is notoriously changeable, and it's usually wise to carry at least a windbreaker. In spring and fall, and even in the summer, low temperatures, cold rain, and a stiff wind can combine to cause hypothermia. Pay attention to weather forecasts, and pack accordingly.

Most bikers have something in which to carry an assortment of the above mentioned items, plus car keys, money, food, perhaps a camera. A backpack is usually a poor choice for biking. It's often uncomfortable, and it raises the rider's center of gravity. Small wedge packs that fit under the bike's seat hold a surprising amount, and they are often all that's needed. Slightly larger packs that attach to the handlebars are popular, and some folks who have a lot to carry or are traveling a longer distance use panniers on a rack.

Other Sources of Information

There are two Vermont road atlases on the market, either of which is a handy complement to this collection: *Vermont Road Atlas and Guide* (Northern Cartographic) and *Vermont Atlas and Gazetteer* (DeLorme). Both include contour lines, which are useful in getting a snapshot of the terrain. They also include information on state parks, historic sites, geologic features, and so on. Both are generally available in book stores, bicycle and sporting goods stores, and even most grocery and general stores in the state. The basic Vermont highway map (free at any Vermont Information Center), although not detailed enough to be of much use on many of the actual rides, will certainly help get you to the starting points.

Vermont Information Centers and local Chambers of Commerce often have brochures suggesting local bike routes, as well as bike clubs and bike shops (always a good source of information). Vermont's Agency of Travel and Tourism (134 State Street, Montpelier, VT, 802–828–3236) can be helpful in suggesting routes, as well as in directing callers to appropriate local resources. Local barracks of the state police are another resource to remember. It's sometimes wise to call the state or local police for a check on road conditions. This is especially true in the spring when washouts can completely close back roads.

Send Suggestions

Conditions change, roads are renamed, and landmarks that are here today may be gone tomorrow. I would appreciate hearing from bikers who have corrections, suggestions, or ideas for other favorite routes. I have a file of possibilities for a next edition and am always on the lookout for a new excursion. Write me in care of The Globe Pequot Press, P.O. Box 833, Old Saybrook, CT 06475.

Vernon
Over the Border, and Welcome Back

Number of Miles:	22.4
Approximate Pedaling Time:	2½ hours
Terrain:	One hill, otherwise flat to gently rolling
Traffic:	Light to moderate
Things to See:	Town of Vernon, Vermont Yankee Nuclear Power Facility, town of Bernardston, MA
Food:	General store and restaurant at parking area on Stebbins Road, general store in Vernon, general stores and restaurants in Bernardston
Facilities:	General store and restaurant at parking area on Stebbins Road

This is a pleasant ride across the border into northern Massachusetts and back. With the exception of the Tyler Hill climb, it's an easy pedal over gently rolling terrain, on roads that are either sparsely traveled or have exceptionally wide shoulders. Be particularly cautious at railroad crossings. The tracks along this route are at oblique angles to the road and can easily catch a wheel. If you can't approach the track at a right angle, it's best to get off and walk across. The route begins just south of Vernon, at a parking pull-off next to the Schoolhouse Grocery and Restaurant, a good stop on either end of the ride.

The Connecticut River was the main thoroughfare for settlers leaving the civilization of southern New England for the wilds of the northern frontier. The Vernon area was the site of Fort Dummer (built in 1724), the first permanent colonial settlement in

1

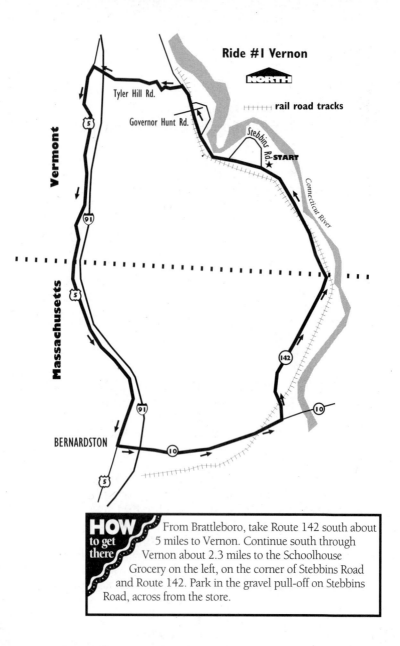

Ride #1 Vernon

NORTH

++++++ **rail road tracks**

Tyler Hill Rd.

Governor Hunt Rd.

Stebbins Rd. ★ START

Connecticut River

Vermont

5

91

Massachusetts

5

91

142

10

BERNARDSTON

10

5

HOW to get there From Brattleboro, take Route 142 south about 5 miles to Vernon. Continue south through Vernon about 2.3 miles to the Schoolhouse Grocery on the left, on the corner of Stebbins Road and Route 142. Park in the gravel pull-off on Stebbins Road, across from the store.

DIREC-TIONS
at a glance

0.0	Turn right out of parking area on Stebbins Road onto Route 142, heading north.
1.3	Governor Hunt Road on right. Optional side trip to Vermont Yankee Nuclear Power Facility. Continue straight on Route 142.
2.3	Town of Vernon. Continue straight on Route 142.
2.5	Cross railroad track. Exercise caution.
2.7	Turn left off Route 142 onto Tyler Hill Road.
4.5	Cross bridge over I–91.
4.9	Junction with Route 5. Turn left onto Route 5, heading south.
8.9	Cross border between Vermont and Massachusetts.
12.8	Junction with Route 10. Turn left off Route 5 onto Route 10 north.
12.9	Town of Bernardston.
13.2	Cross bridge over Falls River.
15.2	Cross bridge over railroad track.
15.6	Turn left off Route 10 onto Route 142 north, following signs for Vernon and Brattleboro.
16.0	Cross railroad track. Exercise caution.
19.6	Cross state line, returning to Vermont.
22.4	Turn right off Route 142 at parking area next to Schoolhouse Grocery.

what is now Vermont. There won't be an opportunity for a side trip to the fort as its site is now underwater behind the Vernon Dam. We can, however, move from colonial camp fires to nuclear energy: At 1.3 miles, a short side trip to the right on Governor Hunt Road brings you to the visitor center of the Vermont Yankee Nuclear Power Facility (open weekdays, free admission).

Watch for the left turn at 2.7 miles onto Tyler Hill Road. The name is a good clue to what's ahead. It's definitely a climb, but not a very long or even a terribly steep one. At 4.5 miles cross

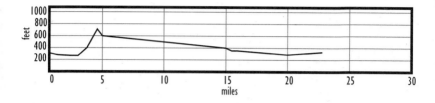

I–91, then begin a very short, but steep and twisting, descent to the junction with Route 5. It's quite clear when you reach Route 5 that the descent you just made wasn't at all comparable to the climb up Tyler Hill. Obviously, there's going to be more downhill before you're back to your starting elevation. And sure enough, the next 8-mile stretch along Route 5 will be a very easy pedal, with the possibility of a lot of gentle coasting. This is a lovely length of biking road: The road has a good surface, the interstate that parallels it bears the burden of the traffic, and the scenery is best described as typical New England as you coast from Vermont into Massachusetts.

Route 10, which takes you east from Bernardston, carries a lot of traffic. However, it has enormous shoulders, is very flat, and is a surprisingly pleasant stretch to pedal. Be particularly careful making the left turn off Route 10 onto Route 142 north. As with any left turn on a busy road, it's best to get off the bike and walk.

Between about 16.3 and 16.7 miles, notice the sand and gravel pits on both sides of the road. You're on a ridge now, which at the end of the last ice age may well have been the western shore of what geologists have named Lake Hitchcock, the long narrow lake formed by the swelling of the Connecticut River, dammed to the south. Sand and gravel companies throughout New England are grateful for the deposits left as the retreating glacier rearranged the New England landscape.

Welcome back to Vermont at 19.6 miles. A couple more miles of easy pedaling and you're back to the parking area on Stebbins Road.

Putney
A Biking Mecca

Number of Miles:	23.1
Approximate Pedaling Time:	3½ hours
Terrain:	Rolling, with one significant climb
Traffic:	Light to moderate
Things to See:	Town of Putney, views of the Connecticut River, village of Westminster
Food:	Putney Food Coop and Deli, stores and restaurants in Putney
Facilities:	Putney Food Coop

Putney is known throughout the state as a sports center—particularly as a center for biking and cross-country skiing. And a lot of that biking and skiing activity seems to touch or be touched by the West Hill Shop, the starting point for this ride. If you have questions about roads, rides, or equipment, this is the place to go. You'll find, too, that the whole Putney area is generally bicycle friendly. The local bike club is big and very active, and local drivers seem accustomed to encountering bikes. They wave and genuinely seem to enjoy having cyclists around. You'll notice on this ride (as of this writing) that one family has put out a water faucet by the side of the road with a sign welcoming bikers to a cold drink. All of Vermont is quite biker friendly, but the Putney-Westminster area wins a top billing in this regard.

Other than in Putney, there are no general stores or restaurants along this route, so plan to bring food and fluid along. The Putney Food Coop and Deli, directly across the street at the turn onto Route 5 (at 0.2 mile) is a good place to stock up. There is also a general store, a bakery, and a restaurant in downtown Putney (at 0.7 mile).

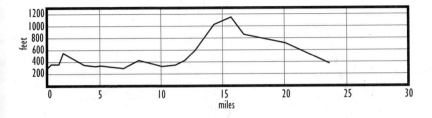

Traffic on Route 5 is moderate. It could be worse: most of the long distance traffic that once traveled Route 5 now uses I–91, which parallels it. But there is still a fair amount of local traffic, so exercise caution. River Road (the right turn off Route 5 at 1.2 miles), in contrast, has almost no traffic, and it offers magnificent views of the Connecticut River. For much of the distance on River Road you'll have the railroad track directly to your right, with the river immediately beyond the track. This is a beautiful stretch of road, where views of the river are obstructed only by areas of trees and fields. The 3.4 miles of dirt surface are flat and well maintained and won't pose a problem for narrow tires. You're back on Route 5 again at 8.2 miles and need to return to more defensive pedaling as traffic increases again. The turn off Route 5 onto Kurn Hattin Road, at 11.1 miles, marks the end of any significant traffic on this trip.

Westminster, where you turn off Route 5, is a historic village. Originally settled in 1735, it was laid out with an unusually straight, wide main street—the "King's Highway." This was the scene of the "Westminster Massacre" in 1775, a skirmish that set the stage for a convention held in Westminster in January 1777, when Vermonters declared their independence from everybody—Britain, New York, and New Hampshire.

Kurn Hattin Road is flat for a short distance but soon begins a 3-mile climb. This is a serious climb, but not relentless. Steeper sections are generally interspersed with gentler ones, so those who elect to get off and do a little walking will probably

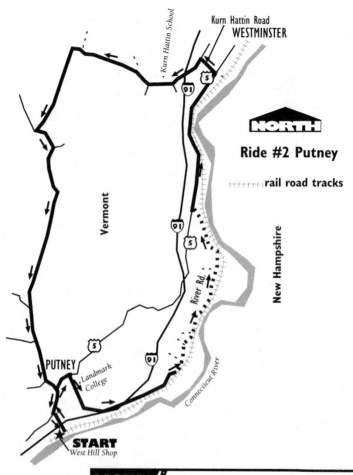

Kurn Hattin School

Kurn Hattin Road
WESTMINSTER

91   5

NORTH

Ride #2 Putney

++++++ **rail road tracks**

Vermont

91

5

New Hampshire

River Rd.

5

91

PUTNEY   Landmark
College

Connecticut River

START
West Hill Shop

HOW
to get
there
From the Brattleboro area, take I–91
north to exit 4. At the end of the exit
ramp, turn right and then make an
immediate right into the entrance to the Green
Mountain Spinnery and West Hill Shop.
Continue straight to the West Hill Bicycle and Ski
Shop at the end of the drive. Park here, out of the way
of regular customer parking.

DIREC-TIONS at a glance

0.0 Turn left out of drive to West Hill Shop.

0.0 Cross bridge over I–91.

0.2 Junction with Route 5. Turn right onto Route 5 north.

0.7 Road forks. Bear right, staying on Route 5 north.

0.8 Cross bridge over Sackett's Brook.

1.2 Turn right off Route 5 onto River Road, following signs for Landmark College.

1.3 Landmark College on left. Continue straight on River Road.

2.9 River Road passes under I–91.

4.5 Dirt road to left. Continue straight on River Road.

4.8 Road surface turns to dirt.

5.0 Dirt road to left (Putney Falls Road). Continue straight on River Road.

6.6 Dirt road to left (Fort Hill Road). Continue straight on River Road.

8.2 Junction with Route 5. Turn right onto Route 5, heading north.

9.7 Paved road to left, which passes under I–91. Continue straight on Route 5.

10.8 Entering village of Westminster.

11.1 Turn left off Route 5 onto Kurn Hattin Road (also called School Street here).

11.4 Pass Westminster School on left.

11.6 Stop sign at junction with another paved road. Turn left, following sign for Kurn Hattin Homes or Kurn Hattin Road.

12.0 Cross bridge over I–91.

12.4 Main entrance to Kurn Hattin School on right.

12.5 Paved road (Piggery Road) to left. Continue straight.

13.9 Sign on right, offering cold water to bikers.

14.7 Road swings sharply to the left.

16.6 Yield sign at junction with another paved road. Sign welcoming to Westminster West. Turn left.
20.4 Cross bridge over Sackett's Brook.
20.5 Hickory Ridge Road (paved) to right. Continue straight.
21.1 Cross Road (paved) to right. Continue straight.
21.2 West Hill Road (paved) to right. Continue straight.
21.4 Putney Central School on left.
22.3 Junction with Route 5. Turn right onto Route 5 south.
22.8 Turn left off Route 5, following signs for I–91 north. (Busy intersection: walk the bike across.)
23.0 Cross bridge over I–91.
23.1 Turn right into driveway for West Hill Shop.

---

be ready to get back on in short order. The water faucet mentioned earlier is at 13.9 miles. It's on the right and is a clear indication that local bikers generally do this loop in this direction—counterclockwise. That faucet wouldn't be nearly as tempting, or even visible, from the other direction. At about 15 miles, you've pretty much reached the top. A little up and down will follow, to be resolved in a very long downhill, with an occasional uphill respite, all the way back to Putney.

Grafton
A Visit to the Nineteenth Century

Number of Miles:	17.5
Approximate Pedaling Time:	2 hours
Terrain:	Hilly
Traffic:	Light to moderate
Things to See:	Village of Grafton, Saxtons River, South Branch Saxtons River, Athens Pond, Grafton Village Cheese Company
Food:	Stores and restaurants in Grafton
Facilities:	Exhibit barn next to Information Building in Grafton

Grafton, our starting point, is a village that requires some explanation. Grafton is perhaps best described as a miniature Williamsburg: Vermont's version of a historical restoration. In the early nineteenth century, Grafton was a thriving town with a population of almost 1,500 people and about 10,000 sheep. By mid-century, strong competition led to a decline in the Vermont wool industry. Many Vermonters moved west, and Grafton, like many Vermont towns, began a general decline. By the 1940s, Grafton's population was a mere 393 people, and most of its buildings had deteriorated badly. In 1963, the Windham Foundation, a philanthropic organization whose first purpose is "to restore buildings and economic vitality in the village of Grafton" was founded. Today the foundation owns about half the buildings and a number of the businesses in town, including the renowned Old Tavern and the Cheese Company. The restorations are beautiful, and Grafton attracts a remarkable number of visitors. Our route begins at the parking area next to the Infor-

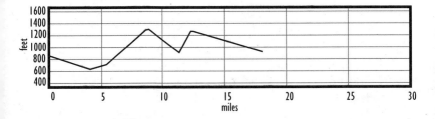

mation Building and adjacent to the Windham Foundation Center. They're both worth a stop.

It's downhill for the first 4 miles. Route 121 follows Saxtons River closely, paralleling its every twist and turn. This road reminds you that the highways in New England are built along what once were footpaths through the wilderness. Over the centuries they've been widened and the surfaces greatly improved, but they still follow the original route, which stuck close to the river.

After the turn onto Route 35, it's a gentle uphill for a little more than a mile. After the fork at 5.5 miles, prepare for a climb. For the next few miles you'll be pedaling through an area that once was much more populated than it is today. You'll pass overgrown pastures, remnants of foundations, and stone walls in what are now mature forests. Notice the handsome brick meeting house on the right at 6.5 miles. It was built in 1817, when Athens was thriving and sheep raising was big business. The ascent is a little more than 2 miles, and includes a mix of steeper and quite gradual sections. The short dirt stretch may provide an opportunity to walk and stretch your legs a bit. You're at the top of the climb at about 8 miles; then it's a long downhill.

Watch carefully for the right turn at 11.0 miles. You could be descending pretty fast at this point, and the turn is immediately after a bend. You'll be turning onto what becomes Townshend Road, but it's unmarked here. (Note that it's the first paved right after the fork at 5.5 miles.) Then it's a serious uphill ride again

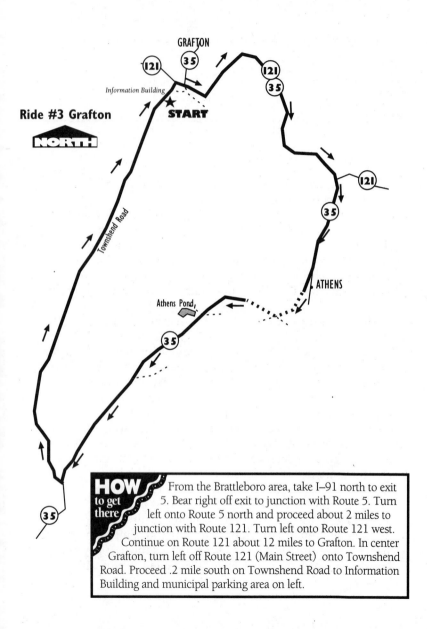

Ride #3 Grafton

NORTH

GRAFTON

START

Information Building

Townshend Road

Athens Pond

ATHENS

HOW to get there From the Brattleboro area, take I–91 north to exit 5. Bear right off exit to junction with Route 5. Turn left onto Route 5 north and proceed about 2 miles to junction with Route 121. Turn left onto Route 121 west. Continue on Route 121 about 12 miles to Grafton. In center Grafton, turn left off Route 121 (Main Street) onto Townshend Road. Proceed .2 mile south on Townshend Road to Information Building and municipal parking area on left.

DIREC-TIONS at a glance

0.0   Turn right out of the Grafton Information Building parking area onto Townshend Road, heading toward Grafton's Main Street.

0.2   Junction with Main Street. Turn right onto Main Street (Route 121 east).

0.3   Cross bridge, pass junction with Route 35 north to left. Continue straight, following signs for Route 121 east.

4.2   Turn right off Route 121 onto Route 35 south.

5.5   Road forks. Bear right, continuing on Route 35, and following signs for Townshend. Begin ascent.

6.1   Road surface turns to dirt.

7.1   Road surface returns to asphalt.

7.7   Athens Pond to the right.

8.2   Approximate top of the watershed. Begin descent.

11.0   Turn right off Route 35 onto the first paved road. (Townshend Road, but unmarked here.) Begin ascent.

12.1   Climb begins to level off.

12.3   Beginning gradual descent to Grafton.

16.9   Grafton Ponds Cross-Country Ski Center on right.

17.1   Grafton Village Cheese Company on right.

17.4   Windham Foundation on right.

17.5   Back to parking area.

for more than 1 mile. The climb levels off gradually, then begin the long gentle descent back to Grafton.

Townshend Road is a wonderful biking road. It's hard to beat 5 miles of gradual descent along a sparsely traveled road with terrific scenery. Once again, the road follows the river very closely. This stream is the South Branch of Saxtons River. It's everything a mountain stream should be: a torrent in the spring, a great place to cool off in summer, an invitation to photograph its collection of colors in the fall.

Plan to stop at the Grafton Village Cheese Company on the right at 17.1 miles. They have a viewing window on the processing areas; and, after 17 miles, the free samples are a treat. The parking area in Grafton is less than .5 miles away, so buying a brick of cheese to carry home won't be a hardship.

Bennington
Backroads of the Revolution

Number of Miles:	13.3
Approximate Pedaling Time:	1¾ hours
Terrain:	Gently rolling
Traffic:	Sparse to moderate
Things to See:	Bennington Museum, Old First Church and cemetery (where Robert Frost is buried), Bennington Battle Monument, Silk Road Covered Bridge, Park McCullough House, Grandma Moses countryside, site of General Stark's camping ground, Henry Covered Bridge, site of Seth Warner's home, site of Breckenridge's farm
Food:	None. Bring water and snacks
Facilities:	Bennington Museum; Bennington Battle Monument visitor center

This ride is an up-close introduction to Vermont history. The route is relatively short and quite flat. The ride could easily be done in an hour and a half, but most riders will want to take longer. Even those with an entrenched resistance to matters historical will find themselves drawn to a stop or two. Follow directions carefully as there are frequent turns and intersections.

The ride begins and ends at the Bennington Museum, whose exhibits include a large collection of Grandma Moses paintings, Bennington pottery and glassware, Revolutionary era artifacts, colonial furniture, and more. Rest rooms and picnic areas are free to the public. There is a moderate admission fee to visit the exhibits.

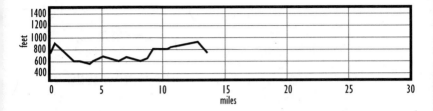

A cautionary note: DO NOT attempt to ride a bike on Route 9. It is an extremely busy road, visibility is poor, and there are no shoulders. From the museum, walk your bike across the road to the sidewalk/bikeway and walk or ride the bike on that (yielding, of course, to the occasional pedestrian). Use the sidewalk/bikeway again when you return from Monument Avenue to the parking area.

At .2 mile Route 9 bears left and our route makes a right onto Monument Avenue. A sharp left here would take you on a short (.1 mile) side trip to the Old First Church and cemetery. The epitaphs are colorful, and there is a well-worn path to Robert Frost's grave.

Many bikers will want to stop at the Bennington Battle Monument. A $1.00 admission fee takes you on an elevator ride to the top (it's a miniature Washington Monument) for a birds-eye view of the terrain you'll be pedaling. The battle actually took place a few miles to the west in New York State; the monument stands on the site of the colonial supply depot, which was the target of the British offensive. Vermont is justifiably proud of the role its largely untrained, but resourceful, troops played in the Revolution. August 16, the date of the battle, is a state holiday.

Our route crosses two covered bridges over the Walloomsac River: the Silk Road Bridge (at 2.4 miles) and the Henry Bridge (at 7.5 miles). Be careful. Both are one lane, so look for oncoming traffic before crossing, and like many covered bridges, both have an awkward gap between the bridge and the pavement, so go slowly.

West St.

Park McCullough
House

Park St.

67A

Harrington Rd.

NORTH

Ride #4 Bennington

67A

Bennington College

67A

Henry Covered Bridge

Murphy Rd.

Silk Road
Covered Bridge

Austin Hill Rd.

Silk Road

Vail Rd.

William H. Morse Airport

Fairview St.

Bennington Battle Monument

Walloomsac Rd.

9

Old First Church

START

9

Bennington Museum

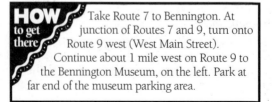

HOW
to get
there
Take Route 7 to Bennington. At junction of Routes 7 and 9, turn onto Route 9 west (West Main Street). Continue about 1 mile west on Route 9 to the Bennington Museum, on the left. Park at far end of the museum parking area.

DIRECTIONS at a glance

0.0 Exit parking area of Bennington Museum, cross Route 9, and proceed left, up the hill, on the sidewalk/bikeway.

0.2 Turn right onto Monument Avenue (the Bennington Battle Monument is clearly visible at end of the street).

0.5 In front of monument and statue of Seth Warner. Turn left onto circular drive, then proceed straight onto Walloomsac Road.

0.6 Three-way stop. Turn right onto Fairview Street.

1.2 Turn right onto Silk Road.

1.8 Silk Road Extension (hard surface) to left. Continue straight on Silk Road.

2.4 Bridge Street (hard surface) to left. Continue straight on Silk Road.

2.4 Cross Silk Road Covered Bridge.

2.6 Stop sign and blinking red light at junction with Route 67A. Entrance to Bennington College is opposite. Turn left onto Route 67A.

3.8 Four-way intersection. Go straight across, onto Hillside Street.

3.9 Yield sign at junction with Park Street. Turn right onto Park Street.

4.1 Road surface turns to hard packed dirt.

4.9 Road surface returns to asphalt.

5.0 Park McCullough House on left.

5.0 Four-way intersection. Turn left onto West Street.

5.4 Road surface turns to hard packed dirt.

6.0 Stop sign at junction with another dirt road. Unlabeled here, this is Harrington Road. Turn left onto Harrington Road.

6.4 Plaque on left marks site of General John Stark's camping ground.

7.0 Road surface returns to asphalt.

7.5 Turn right off Harrington Road and immediately cross Henry Covered Bridge. Road forks immediately after the bridge. Bear left on Murphy Road.

7.8 Plaque on right marks site of Revolutionary hero Seth Warner's home.

8.0 Plaque on left marks site of Breckenridge's Farm.

8.2 Make right off Murphy Road onto Austin Hill Road. Begin short ascent up Austin Hill.

8.6 Top of Austin Hill. Continue straight.

9.1 Stop sign at junction with another hard surface road (Vail Road). Turn right.

9.7 Road makes a sharp left.

10.5 Stop sign. Turn left onto Walloomsac Road.

11.0 Dermody Road enters from the right. Continue straight on Walloomsac Road.

11.1 Entrance to William H. Morse airport on left. Continue straight.

12.0 Road appears to fork. Bear left, continuing on Walloomsac Road.

12.6 Three-way stop. Fairview Street is to the left. Continue straight on Walloomsac.

12.7 Junction with circular drive around monument. Continue straight, then make an immediate right onto Monument Avenue.

13.1 Stop sign at junction with Route 9. Turn left onto sidewalk/bikeway paralleling Route 9.

13.3 Cross Route 9 and return to museum parking area.

The Park McCullough House (at 5.0 miles) will interest historians of the Victorian era. It's an elegantly preserved mansion, originally built as a summer home, with groomed grounds and Victorian gardens (moderate admission fee).

There are two sections of this route that are on dirt roads (total of 2.4 miles). Both sections are hard packed gravel and offer easy backroad pedaling suitable for even the skinniest tires. During the second section of dirt road, at about 6.2 miles, notice the views of New York State in the distance to the right. That's Hoosick, New York, best known as Grandma Moses country. Also on this dirt stretch, at 6.4 miles, is a stone marker commemorating General John Stark's camping ground, August 14–16, 1777. Students of Vermont history will be pleased to find, just a little farther along, the sites of Seth Warner's home and of Breckenridge's farm, where, in 1771, Vermonters fought for independence from New York.

Arlington
The Batten Kill Tour

Number of Miles:	12.1
Approximate Pedaling Time:	1¾ hours
Terrain:	Mostly level
Traffic:	Moderate to light
Things to See:	Batten Kill River, West Arlington Covered Bridge
Food:	Wayside Country Store at 3.1 miles

This is an easy pedal along the beautiful valley cut by the Batten Kill River through the Taconic Mountains. You'll be a stone's throw from the river for nearly the whole trip. On a hot day, you'll certainly want to take advantage of opportunities for a swim or a rest by the river. About half the ride is on a dirt road, which, although a good hard packed surface, necessitates a more leisurely pace. This isn't the trip for those committed to speed or hill climbing, but for those interested in a gentle pedal with lovely views, this ride is a winner.

The route begins at a public parking area off Route 313, at the edge of the Batten Kill River. The Batten Kill is a popular fishing, canoeing, and tubing river. This parking area is the put-in for a favorite stretch of canoeing. The Batten Kill flows swiftly over a rocky riverbed, and its water is unusually clear. There are no major rapids, but the current is fast enough to make for an interesting paddle. On a hot weekend, boat traffic on the river seems nearly equal to auto traffic on the road. In the early morning, fishermen will probably outnumber the paddlers. The Batten Kill is a world-renowned trout stream and is a mecca for fly fishermen. The river isn't particularly wide, and it can be inter-

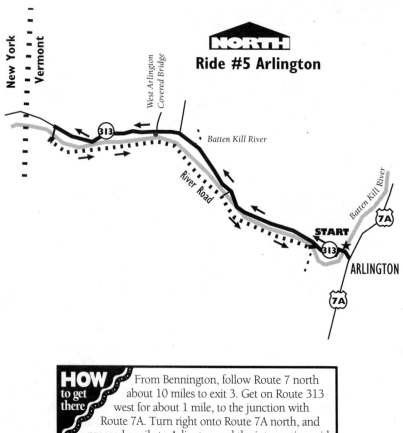

NORTH

Ride #5 Arlington

New York
Vermont

West Arlington
Covered Bridge

313

Batten Kill River

River Road

Batten Kill River

START
313

7A

ARLINGTON

7A

HOW to get there   From Bennington, follow Route 7 north about 10 miles to exit 3. Get on Route 313 west for about 1 mile, to the junction with Route 7A. Turn right onto Route 7A north, and proceed a mile to Arlington and the intersection with Route 313 west. Turn left off Route 7A onto Route 313 west. Proceed .2 mile to the public parking area on the right, next to the river. Park here.

DIREC-TIONS at a glance

0.0 Exit parking area next to Batten Kill River. Turn right onto Route 313 heading west.

0.1 Cross bridge over the Batten Kill.

0.5 Bridge to left over the Batten Kill. Continue straight on Route 313.

2.5 Bridge to left over the Batten Kill. Continue straight on Route 313.

3.1 Wayside Country Store on left.

3.7 Sandgate Road (paved) to the right. Continue straight on Route 313.

4.0 Covered bridge over the Batten Kill to the left. Continue straight on Route 313.

5.8 Turn left off Route 313 onto River Road (a dirt road).

5.9 Cross bridge over the Batten Kill. River Road swings left and heads east along the Batten Kill.

7.8 Bear left onto Covered Bridge Road to visit bridge and swimming hole.

7.9 Covered Bridge and swimming hole. Turn around to return to River Road.

8.0 Bear left off Covered Bridge Road onto River Road again.

9.5 Benedict Crossing Road to left. Continue straight on River Road.

9.8 Benedict Hollow Road to right. Continue straight on River Road.

11.4 Hollerith Road to right. Continue straight on River Road.

11.5 Road surface returns to asphalt. River Road crosses bridge over the Batten Kill.

11.6 Stop sign at junction with Route 313. Turn right onto Route 313, heading east.

12.0 Cross bridge over Batten Kill.

12.1 Return to parking area.

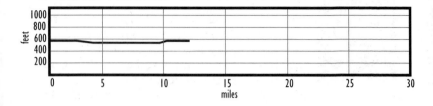

esting to watch the fishermen and the paddlers jockeying for space.

The first half of the ride is on Route 313, heading west. It's a narrow valley, and Route 313 twists and turns along with the river. The road itself is fairly narrow, and there is some traffic. Exercise caution. There are a number of pull-offs where fishermen park. You'll want to stop occasionally in order to devote attention to the scenery. Unlike the Green Mountains to the east, which seem a high solid wall, the Taconic Range tends more toward peaks and valleys.

Turn left off Route 313 at 5.8 miles, cross the Batten Kill, and begin heading back along the south side of the river. The road surface is dirt now. The pace has to slow down, but traffic is very sparse and views of the river are lovely. Again, there are a number of fishermen's pull-offs, which are also handy for bikers. Do be respectful of private property and NO TRESPASSING signs.

Our route contains a short (.1 mile) side trip to the West Arlington Covered Bridge. This is one of the most frequently photographed bridges in the state. You may recognize it from the calendar in your kitchen. Attractive as they are, the calendar photos usually don't capture one of the bridge's most popular features: the picnic spot and swimming hole beside it. Bikers, paddlers, and tubers often stop here to swim and to lounge on the grass.

After the side trip to the bridge, our route returns to River Road, which continues to parallel the river until crossing back to Route 313. Then it's just a short distance back to the parking area.

This is a beautiful part of Vermont, and a short ride like this may whet your appetite for more. Unfortunately, there aren't many safe short loops in this area of the state. The valley between the Green Mountains and the Taconics is narrow in southern Vermont; and Route 7 (or 7A) is the major, usually the only, north-south route. Because of heavy traffic and lack of shoulders, bikers are advised to avoid Routes 7 and 7A. Those committed to more biking in the area will find that there are a number of possible short "out and back" trips. For some folks, mountain biking on the steeper dirt roads to the east is another alternative.

Pawlet/Rupert/ West Pawlet
Using All Your Gears in the Taconics

Number of Miles:	25.8
Approximate Pedaling Time:	3½ hours
Terrain:	Varied, from unusually flat to steep
Traffic:	Moderate to light
Things to See:	Town of Pawlet, Mettawee River, Taconic Mountain Range, D & H rail trail, slate quarries
Food:	Restaurant and general store in Pawlet, general store in West Pawlet

There is more variety of terrain in this ride than in almost any other in this collection. It's a wonderful route and will be a favorite among dedicated bikers. For weekend riders, however, the steep section over the Taconics might make this a poor choice for a first ride of the season. This is a lesser-known corner of Vermont. You'll see some elegantly restored farmhouses, but it's also an area where farming and slate quarrying are still important and where the general stores aren't just for the tourists—they're the real thing.

Begin in the village of Pawlet, a farming town that, in recent years, has become home to an assortment of craftsmen and artists (look for signs). Don't miss the view of the river through the hole in the floor of Mach's Store.

From the parking area, return to Route 30, and head south. You'll be following, and occasionally crossing, the Mettawee River, passing through the rich farmlands of its beautiful valley.

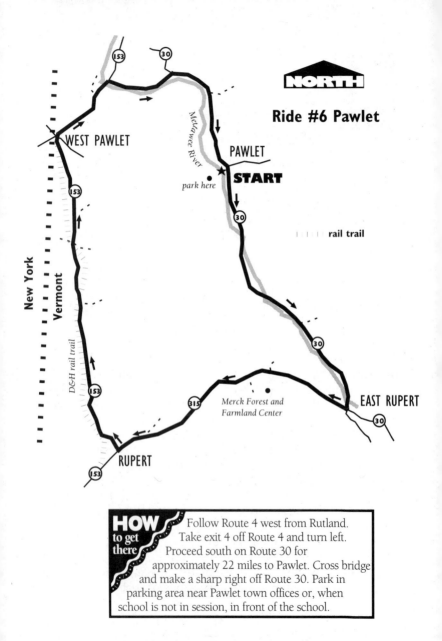

NORTH

Ride #6 Pawlet

153
30

WEST PAWLET

Mettawee River

PAWLET

START

park here

153

30

| | | | **rail trail**

New York

Vermont

D&H rail trail

153

315

Merck Forest and Farmland Center

EAST RUPERT

30

153

RUPERT

153

HOW to get there Follow Route 4 west from Rutland. Take exit 4 off Route 4 and turn left. Proceed south on Route 30 for approximately 22 miles to Pawlet. Cross bridge and make a sharp right off Route 30. Park in parking area near Pawlet town offices or, when school is not in session, in front of the school.

DIREC-TIONS at a glance

0.0	Park in Pawlet near school and town offices. Return to Route 30.
0.1	Turn right onto Route 30 south.
1.6	Bridge over Mettawee River.
3.2	Another bridge over Mettawee River.
4.6	Department of Fish and Wildlife's Mettawee River Access Area on right.
6.3	East Rupert. Turn right onto Route 315 west. Begin ascent.
8.9	Reach highest elevation. Begin descent.
12.3	Village of Rupert. Route 315 ends. Turn right onto Route 153 north.
12.8	Rail trail option for riders with mountain or hybrid bikes.
15.6	Rail trail crosses road.
16.4	Leave Rupert, Bennington County. Enter West Pawlet, Rutland County.
16.9	Rail trail crosses again.
19.3	Village of West Pawlet. Bear right to continue on Route 153 north.
21.3	Cross bridge over Mettawee River. Road forks. Bear right.
22.9	Junction with Route 30. Turn right.
25.7	Return to Pawlet. Cross bridge and bear right past Mach's Store.
25.8	Back to parking area.

This is a rare opportunity to put your bike in high gear, and leave it there for several miles. You're actually going uphill, but it's so gradual and so straight that it feels flat.

At 6.3 miles you're in East Rupert and about to turn west onto Route 315. It's time to start downshifting, as it's going to be relentlessly uphill for the next 2.5 miles. You'll be ascending about 800 feet in elevation. Long uphills like this can be tough

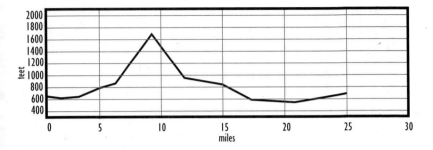

on the knees, not to mention out-of-shape muscles. There's no disgrace in giving your legs a break by getting off and walking. Also, there are fine views to the east, which you won't appreciate unless you get off and look behind. You'll reach the crest at 8.9 miles. The entrance to the Merck Forest and Farmland Center, a nature study center, is to the left (.5 mile up a dirt road). You can upshift now, or leave it in low. It doesn't matter, as brakes will be all you'll need till Rupert.

Don't miss the post office on your left in the village of Rupert. You're unlikely, in your travels, to see one that's smaller.

Notice the rail trail to your left at about 12.8 miles. It isn't marked, but it is clearly identifiable as the old D & H railroad bed turned recreational path. If you have fat tires you may want to leave the road now and hop on the rail trail, which parallels the road closely from here to West Pawlet. Traffic is sparse on Route 153, so the biggest advantage of the rail trail is its remarkable flatness. If you stay on the road, you'll notice the rail trail cross your path twice before you get to West Pawlet.

At 19.3 miles you're in the village of West Pawlet, at the intersection of five roads (and the rail trail). Bear right, continuing on Route 153 north. If you're ready for a snack, the general store in West Pawlet is directly across the intersection.

As you leave West Pawlet, note the slag heaps and quarry holes. West Pawlet is part of a slate belt, which includes a narrow area of eastern New York and western Vermont. You may have noticed Welsh family names, perhaps on mailboxes. Many residents are descendants of Welshmen who came to the area in the late nineteenth century to work in the slate quarries.

At 22.9 miles, at the junction with Route 30, turn right and begin to encounter a bit more traffic. You're back in the Mettawee Valley, and it's less than 3 miles back to Pawlet.

Poultney/Middletown/ Wells
The Best of the West

Number of Miles:	26.4
Approximate Pedaling Time:	3½ hours
Terrain:	Rolling hills, with one long downhill
Traffic:	Light to moderate
Things to See:	Town of Poultney, Poultney farmers' market on Thursdays in summer, East Poultney green and museums, Middletown's Mineral Springs Park, Lake St. Catherine, Lake St. Catherine State Park
Food:	Restaurants and convenience stores in Poultney, East Poultney General Store, general stores in Middletown Springs and Wells, store at Lake St. Catherine State Park
Facilities:	Lake St. Catherine State Park

West central Vermont, known as the "Lakes Region," is a wonderful place to bike. Scenery is excellent, terrain is rolling without being tortuous, traffic is usually moderate, general stores are friendly, and there are lots of places to stop for a swim, a glimpse of history, or a rest by a stream. The area has a flavor of the "real" Vermont, where people take pride in a rural way of life.

Begin in Poultney, at the junction of Depot and Main Streets. Head east on Main Street (Route 140) to the village of East Poultney at 1.7 miles. The colonial church on the green in East Poultney may be the most frequently photographed church in

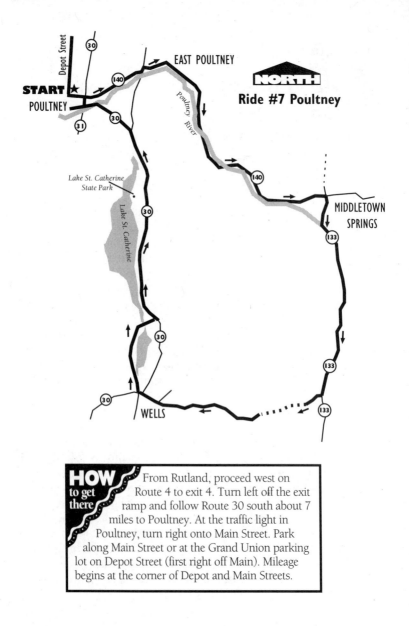

Depot Street

30

EAST POULTNEY

NORTH

Ride #7 Poultney

140

START ★

POULTNEY

31

30

Poultney River

140

Lake St. Catherine
State Park

30

MIDDLETOWN
SPRINGS

133

Lake St. Catherine

30

133

30

30

133

WELLS

133

HOW From Rutland, proceed west on
to get Route 4 to exit 4. Turn left off the exit
there ramp and follow Route 30 south about 7
miles to Poultney. At the traffic light in
Poultney, turn right onto Main Street. Park
along Main Street or at the Grand Union parking
lot on Depot Street (first right off Main). Mileage
begins at the corner of Depot and Main Streets.

0.0 Junction Depot and Main Streets. Head east on Main Street (Route 140).

0.2 Traffic light. Continue east on Route 140.

1.7 East Poultney town green and four corners. Continue straight on Route 140.

8.4 Intersection Route 140 and Route 133 in Middletown Springs. Turn right onto Route 133, heading south.

13.4 Turn right onto hard-surface road following signs to Wells and Lake St. Catherine (will be first hard-surface right off Route 133).

14.0 Road surface changes to hard packed dirt.

14.7 Road surface returns to asphalt. Begin long downhill.

18.1 Stop sign at junction with Route 30. Go left, then take an immediate right next to the Wells post office.

20.1 Stop sign. Turn right.

20.2 Cross bridge over channel between northern and southern sections of the lake.

20.3 Junction with Route 30. Turn left onto Route 30 heading north.

22.8 Entrance to Lake St. Catherine State Park on left.

25.8 Bridge over Poultney River. Route 30 makes sharp left.

26.1 Blinking light. Turn right.

26.2 Traffic light. Turn left onto Main Street.

26.4 Return to start.

---

the state. In fact, the whole village seems an invitation to photographers. East Poultney was the original Poultney and was home to both Horace Greeley (founder of the *New York Herald Tribune*) and George Jones (co-founder of the *New York Times*). East Poultney also claims to be the site of the first public library in Vermont. On Sunday afternoons in summer, three museums on the green are open for tours.

As you continue east on Route 140, you'll follow the Poult-

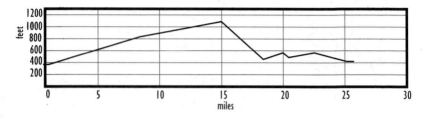

ney River. Locals have several favorite swimming holes here.
Stop to cool your feet and admire the river, but do be respectful
of No Trespassing signs. Burnham Hollow Orchard, on the right
at 6.9 miles, is a good short side trip in the fall for apples and
cider. At 8.4 miles, reach the town of Middletown Springs. As
the name suggests, Middletown was a resort spa during the late
nineteenth century. Visit the Mineral Springs Park by taking an
optional left off Route 133 at 8.5 miles.

Route 133 south of Middletown Springs follows a beautiful
valley of the Taconic Range. This is the quintessential Vermont
bike route: farmhouses, cows, mountain views, sparse traffic,
pleasant road surface, and a very gradual rolling ascent. Relax,
breathe deeply, enjoy the scenery. Biking doesn't get much better
than this.

Watch carefully for the right turn off Route 133 at 13.4
miles. Road signs will point to Wells and Lake St. Catherine. At
14.0 miles the road turns to hard packed dirt for a short stretch.
Then it's time to check your brakes, as it's downhill for the next
3.4 miles, all the way to Wells.

Come to a stop sign in Wells, at the junction with Route 30.
Wells has two thriving general stores. You might want to stop at
both: ice cream at one and soda at the other. At the intersection
you'll make a left onto Route 30, then an immediate right. Now
you'll be heading north along the west shore of Lake St. Catherine.

Lake St. Catherine is really two lakes connected by a narrow
channel. The southern part, which you see first, is shallower

40

and slightly less populated. You'll cross the channel at 20.2 miles and begin heading north along the east shore of the northern section of the lake. Be especially cautious for the next few miles. Route 30 is more heavily traveled (especially in summer) than other roads on this trip, and it's narrow. At 22.8 miles, Route 30 sprouts wide shoulders, and you come to the entrance to the Lake St. Catherine State Park ($1.50 admission, picnic areas, beach). It's a beautiful lake and well worth a stop at the state park. Cross the Poultney River again at 25.8 miles, and you're back in the town of Poultney.

Castleton/Hubbardton
The Battlefield Loop

Number of Miles:	20.9
Approximate Pedaling Time:	3 hours
Terrain:	Hilly
Traffic:	Light for most of trip, moderate on Route 30
Things to See:	Castleton architecture, Hubbardton Battlefield, Lake Bomoseen
Food:	General stores and restaurants in Castleton, general stores on Route 30
Facilities:	Hubbardton Battlefield visitor center

Castleton, our starting point, is just about what comes to mind when you envision a small New England college town: wide main street, colonial homes, brick public library, a village store. Castleton also has some significant architectural landmarks. Thomas Dake, an early-nineteenth-century house joiner, lived in Castleton and built a number of its most handsome buildings. Notice the Langdon-Cole House directly across the street as you turn onto Route 4A at 0.3 miles and the Greek Revival-style Federated Church, on the left at 0.5 miles.

After making the left off Route 4A and crossing Route 4, you're on the East Hubbardton Road. It will be gradually uphill to the Hubbardton Battlefield, with a short steep section just before the top of Monument Hill. The East Hubbardton Road crosses Brittain Brook and its tributaries several times and offers typical Vermont farm scenery. The swimming hole on the left at 2.1 miles may be tempting on a hot day. Between about 3.9 and 4.9 miles, notice the television and radio tower on your right.

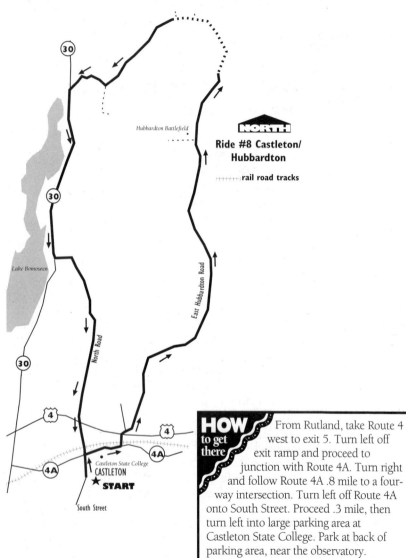

30

30

Hubbardton Battlefield

NORTH

**Ride #8 Castleton/
Hubbardton**

┊┊┊┊┊┊ **rail road tracks**

30

Lake Bomoseen

30

East Hubbardton Road

North Road

4

4

4A

4A

Castleton State College
CASTLETON
★ **START**

South Street

**HOW
to get
there**   From Rutland, take Route 4 west to exit 5. Turn left off exit ramp and proceed to junction with Route 4A. Turn right and follow Route 4A .8 mile to a four-way intersection. Turn left off Route 4A onto South Street. Proceed .3 mile, then turn left into large parking area at Castleton State College. Park at back of parking area, near the observatory.

DIREC-TIONS at a glance

0.0 Turn right out of parking area onto South Street.

0.3 Stop sign. Turn right onto Main Street (Route 4A), heading east.

0.5 Federated Church of Castleton on left.

1.0 Turn left off Route 4A, following signs for Route 4.

1.1 Cross railroad track and bridge over Castleton River.

1.2 Cross Route 4.

1.3 Hard-surface road enters from left. Continue straight, following signs for Hubbardton.

7.6 Entrance to Hubbardton Battlefield on left.

8.8 Road surface turns to dirt.

10.3 Dirt road to the right. Continue straight.

10.6 Dirt road to right. Continue straight.

10.8 Road surface returns to asphalt.

13.3 Stop sign at junction with Route 30. Turn left onto Route 30 heading south.

15.0 Pumpkin Patch Country Store on right.

15.5 Hard surface road to right. Continue straight on Route 30.

16.5 Turn left off Route 30 onto North Road. Lakeside Country Store on corner.

18.4 Highest elevation on North Road.

20.0 Cross Route 4.

20.4 Cross Castleton River.

20.5 Cross railroad track.

20.6 Stop sign at junction of North Road and Route 4A. Cross Route 4A onto South Street.

20.9 Make left off South Street into parking area.

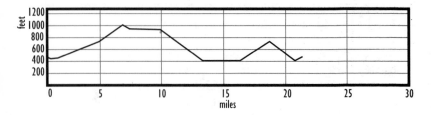

It's on top of Grandpa's Knob, the site of an experimental World War II era wind generator. The windmill's success ended only when it blew apart in 1945.

The Hubbardton Battlefield is a state-owned historical site. It's at the top of Monument Hill, with magnificent views to the south and east. Bikers are welcome to use picnic areas and rest rooms (nominal admission fee to tour the site). Hubbardton was the only Revolutionary War battle fought entirely in Vermont. It is described by the state's Division for Historic Preservation as "one of the most successful rearguard actions in the annals of American military history." It was here that the British caught up with American forces who were retreating after the loss of Fort Ticonderoga. Although it is generally considered a defeat for the colonists, historians are quick to point out the skill and courage with which the Vermonters delayed the British and pre-served the main American force, setting the stage for victory at Bennington and for the British surrender at Saratoga. Each July, a reenactment commemorates the battle.

The battlefield is the highest point of the ride. About 1 mile after starting down the other side of Monument Hill, the road surface turns to hard packed dirt, and remains dirt for the next 2 miles. The dirt portion is very flat, with an extensive swampy area to the left. Naturalists may want to spend some time spot-ting birds and other wildlife.

At about 11.6 miles, begin a long downhill. Portions of the next couple of miles are very steep and winding. Use your brakes, stopping occasionally for views of the Adirondacks and

Lake Bomoseen to the west. Be ready for the stop sign at 13.3 miles: it's after a sharp right and if not careful, you could be rolling too fast to stop.

Route 30 is a busier road, especially in summer, when cottages along Lake Bomoseen are in use. The north end of the lake is shallow and swampy and is especially beautiful in the early fall, when colors can be startlingly intense. Watch carefully for the left turn at 16.5 miles. You'll be turning onto North Road, which will be the first paved left. The Lakeside Country Store on the corner of Route 30 and North Road is a good landmark, and a good place to refuel. Although not terribly steep, the first couple of miles of North Road are uphill and are going to require some reserve energy. The crest of North Road is at about 18.4 miles. Then it's a glorious downhill back to Castleton.

Fair Haven/Lake Bomoseen/Glen Lake
A Lakes and Slate Tour

Number of Miles:	12
Approximate Pedaling Time:	1½ hours
Terrain:	Rolling hills
Traffic:	Light, except along Lake Bomoseen in summer
Things to See:	Town of Fair Haven, Lake Bomoseen, Lake Bomoseen State Park, Glen Lake, slate quarries, Adirondack views
Food:	Restaurants and convenience stores in Fair Haven, general store at south end of Lake Bomoseen, Lake Bomoseen State Park
Facilities:	Lake Bomoseen State Park

Fair Haven is a typical Vermont community with a lively history and an impressive town green. A founder of the town was "Spitting" Matt Lyon, a radical congressman who was imprisoned because of his criticism of President John Adams. Slate quarrying was, and still is, an important industry here. Notice the handsome slate roofs in town and throughout your tour of the area.

Leave your car in the public parking lot at the west end of the town green. On Fridays in summer, the green becomes a traditional farmers' market—fresh produce, baked goods, crafts, and a pleasant way to begin or end a ride. Head west on Main Street (Route 4A/22A) for about .1 mile, making a left onto River Street. Continue on River Street until you reach a stop sign

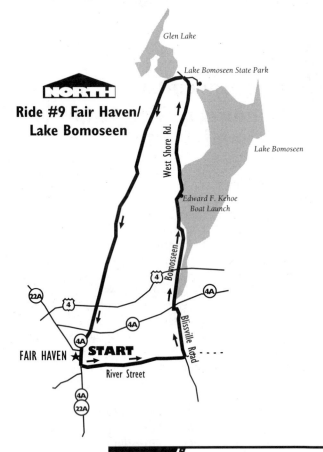

Glen Lake

Lake Bomoseen State Park

NORTH

Ride #9 Fair Haven/ Lake Bomoseen

West Shore Rd.

Lake Bomoseen

Edward F. Kehoe Boat Launch

Bomoseen

4

22A 4

4A

4A

4A

Blissville Road

FAIR HAVEN ★ **START**

River Street

4A

22A

HOW to get there From Rutland, proceed west on Route 4 to exit 2. Turn left off the exit ramp onto Route 22A, following signs for Fair Haven. Go south less than 1 mile to the intersection with Route 4A. Bear right onto Route 4A, which is Fair Haven's Main Street. The town green will be on your right. Continue to the west (far) end of the town green and park in the public lot.

DIREC-TIONS at a glance

0.0	Public parking lot at west end of town green. Turn right onto Main Street (Route 4A/22A).
0.1	Turn left off Main Street onto River Street.
1.9	Stop sign. Turn left onto Blissville Road.
2.7	Intersection with Route 4A. Turn left onto Route 4A, then make an immediate right onto Bomoseen West Shore Road.
4.7	Edward F. Kehoe boat launch.
6.7	Entrance to Bomoseen State Park.
6.7	Entrance to Glen Lake boat launch.
7.0	Glen Lake syncline (rock formation) on right.
7.6	Working slate quarry.
11.5	Intersection with Route 4A. Turn right onto Route 4A, heading west.
12.0	Back to parking lot.

(at 1.9 miles). Turn left and continue to the intersection with Route 4A, at 2.7 miles. Go left, and make an immediate right onto the Bomoseen West Shore Road.

For the next few miles you'll be heading north along the west shore of the lake, with cottages to your left and water to your right. There's some controversy over the origin of the lake's name. It sounds like a variation on an Indian name, but some feel certain that Samuel de Champlain called it "Bombazon," after a silky cloth which the lake's smooth surface resembled. In any case, local residents like to point out that Bomoseen is the largest lake entirely within the boundaries of Vermont. During the summer, cottages will be occupied and there will be traffic, but you won't see much activity on or around the lake during the rest of the year. The Edward F. Kehoe boat launch, at 4.7 miles, is a good place to stop for a break and to admire the view. Notice the island to the north. That's Neshobe Island, formerly owned

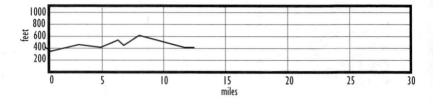

by Alexander Woollcott, who vacationed there with an assortment of zany celebrity friends, including the Marx Brothers.

Continue on the hard-surface road as it travels up the lake shore and then veers west, away from the water. At 6.7 miles you'll come to the entrance to Bomoseen State Park. It's open mid-May through Columbus Day ($1.50 admission, beach, bath houses, concession stand). If you're not ready for an official beach stop but would like a quick dip or a rest by the water, continue about 50 yards to a dirt road to the right, which leads to the boat launch on Glen Lake. People picnic and swim from the shore to the right of the boat launch. During midweek, even on the hottest days, it's often remarkably empty. As you leave Glen Lake (same way you came in), notice the remains of a slate milling factory and foundations of the cottages where factory workers lived. This area was once the town of West Castleton and the center of a thriving slate business.

Get back on the hard-surface road, and almost immediately on the right (at 7.0 miles), look for an impressive rock formation—an overturned syncline. It's a classic example of folded layers, and geology classes from near and far seem delighted with it. You'll continue along the shore of Glen Lake for a bit, and then climb a short hill. At about 7.6 miles you'll pass a working slate quarry. Later on you'll see slag heaps (piles of discarded slate) to your right. Most are from quarries that have long been closed. At about 10 miles you'll begin to see views of the Adirondacks to the west. A wonderful panorama any time of year, it's spectacular on a clear fall day. A long rolling descent returns you to Fair Haven.

Fair Haven/West Haven
Vermont to New York Loop

Number of Miles:	14.8
Approximate Pedaling Time:	2 hours
Terrain:	Rolling hills
Traffic:	Sparse, except on Route 22A where it will be moderate
Things to See:	Views of Adirondack, Taconic, and Green Mountains, Poultney River, William Miller Chapel National Historical Site
Food:	Restaurants, grocery store in Fair Haven

Hills are the theme of this ride: not big mountains, and not long unrelenting climbs—just wonderfully rolling hills. Serious riders love to do this route for speed, relishing the opportunities for short bursts of hill climbing. Weekend riders love it, too, but at a more relaxed pace, with stops for scenery and perhaps with a preference for the exhilarating downhills. Except on Route 22A, traffic is sparse, and road surfaces are excellent. This route is just plain fun to pedal.

Begin at the McDonald's north of Fair Haven and head north on Route 22A. Route 22A is a major north-south artery, and, by Vermont standards, traffic is heavy. This stretch, however, is quite straight and has unusually wide shoulders. If not ideal, it's at least acceptable biking. At 2.6 miles, turn left off Route 22A (first left onto a hard-surface road). This is Main Road, in the town of West Haven, and that's the West Haven School on the left immediately after the turn. Traffic will be minimal now until

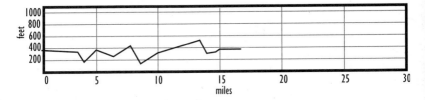

you return to Fair Haven. And the hills will begin.

At 4.8 miles, notice the cemetery on the left. It's a classic old Vermont cemetery and a good rest stop. Some of the markers date from the 1790s. Today this cemetery seems to be in the middle of nowhere, but there was once a larger community here. If you look carefully, you'll notice traces of old foundations as you pedal along.

At 6.0 miles make a left onto Book Road (first asphalt road on the left) and immediately pass the West Haven Baptist Church on the right. It's uphill for a while, then, at about 7.2 miles, you begin the magnificent descent into the Poultney River Valley. In the near distance to the east are Vermont's Taconic Mountains. The Green Mountains are in the far distance.

Cross a bridge over the Poultney River at 8.2 miles and enter New York State. The Poultney River has been designated a State Outstanding Resource Water. A significant portion of the river bank between here and Lake Champlain (about 8 miles) is now held by the Vermont and New York Nature Conservancies and is home to an unusual variety of wildlife.

At 9.0 miles make a left onto an asphalt road, following signs for Fair Haven. The hills continue, with a bit more up than down for the next couple miles.

Reach the crest of a hill at 11.4 miles, and plan to take a few minutes to admire the panorama of Vermont to the east. In summer, it's obvious from here why Vermont is called The Green Mountain state. You're really not terribly high (elevation about 530 feet), but it feels as though western Vermont is stretched out at your feet.

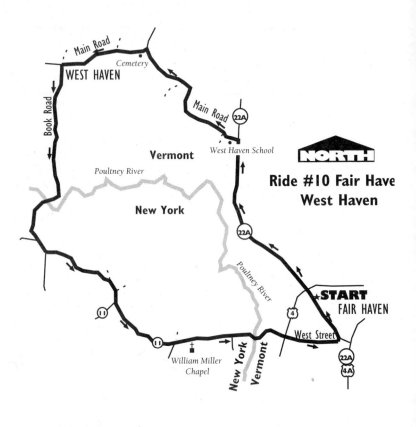

WEST HAVEN

Main Road

Cemetery

Book Road

Main Road

22A

Vermont

West Haven School

Poultney River

NORTH

Ride #10 Fair Haven
West Haven

New York

11

22A

Poultney River

4

★**START**
FAIR HAVEN

West Street

11

William Miller
Chapel

New York
Vermont

22A
4A

HOW
to get
there
From Rutland, take Route 4 west to
exit 2 and Route 22A. Follow Route
22A south toward Fair Haven. Make an
immediate left off Route 22A at the
McDonald's. Park in the large parking area to
the rear or, on weekends, in the area adjacent to
the bank next door.

0.0	Turn right out of McDonald's parking lot, heading north on Route 22A.
2.6	Turn left off Route 22A, onto Main Road (unmarked, first hard-surface left).
2.7	Pass West Haven School on left.
3.9	Cross bridge over Hubbardton River.
4.7	Road forks. Bear left, continuing on Main Road.
4.8	Old cemetery on left.
6.0	Left turn off Main Road onto Book Road.
7.2	Start descent to Poultney River.
8.2	Cross bridge over Poultney River.
8.8	Hard-surface road joins Book Road from right. Pass cemetery on right.
9.0	Turn left onto hard-surface road, following signs for Fair Haven.
10.4	Road forks. Bear left.
11.4	Crest of hill. Great views.
11.7	William Miller Chapel Historical Site on right.
12.7	Cross bridge over Poultney River and reenter Vermont.
13.3	Cross bridge over Route 4.
14.1	Stop sign. Make sharp left onto Route 22A north.
14.8	Return to McDonald's parking lot.

The William Miller Chapel National Historical Site is on your right at 11.7 miles. William Miller was founder of the Millerites, an adventist religious group during the mid-nineteenth century and precursor of today's Seventh Day Adventists. Miller and his followers predicted that the world would end on October 22, 1844. It didn't, but William Miller and his chapel are a colorful square in the patchwork of the area's history.

Another bridge over the Poultney River at 12.7 mile brings you back into Vermont and to the outskirts of Fair Haven.

Orwell/Lake Champlain/ Shoreham
In Ethan Allen's Footsteps

Number of Miles: 20.0
Approximate Pedaling Time: 2½ hours (more if Fort Ticonderoga or Mount Independence are included)
Terrain: Gently rolling, open
Traffic: Light
Things to See: Farms and orchards, Lake Champlain ferry, Larrabee's Point, Fort Ticonderoga
Food: General store in Orwell, Larrabee's Point Store, general store in Shoreham

This part of the state is open and rolling. For those who combine their love of biking with an interest in colonial history, this is a perfect ride. The trip as written takes you to the shore of Lake Champlain. It can be extended by taking the ferry across to New York State and visiting Fort Ticonderoga (2–3 additional miles and an additional hour or two to tour the fort). Those looking for a longer trip, and a two-fort tour, might consider a first side trip to the new visitor center at Mount Independence. Mount Independence was an American fort built directly across from Fort Ticonderoga, on the eastern shore of Lake Champlain. At one time the two forts were connected by a floating bridge. To get to Mount Independence continue straight instead of bearing right at .6 miles. The total round trip to Mount Independence would add approximately nine miles to this ride.

For the first six miles you'll pass through some of Vermont's

Ride #11 Orwell

NORTH

SHOREHAM

Lake Champlain

Larrabee's
Point

ferry

Fort Ticonderoga

Mount Independence

Richville Pond

START

ORWELL

HOW to get there Proceed west from Rutland on Route 4. Take exit 2 onto Route 22A, heading north. Continue north on Route 22A about 15 miles to the intersection with Route 73. Turn right onto Route 73, reaching Orwell in .3 mile. Park to the left, off Route 73, in front of the Orwell school and town offices and across from the general store.

DIREC-TIONS at a glance

0.0 Parking area in front of Orwell school and town offices. Turn right, heading west on Route 73

0.3 Cross Route 22A, continuing on Route 73.

0.6 Road forks. Bear right, continuing on Route 73.

6.1 Junction with Route 74. Turn left onto Route 74, heading west.

6.6 Road ends. Optional ferry crossing to New York. Turn around and head east on Route 74.

7.1 Pass junction with Route 73. Continue straight on Route 74.

7.9 Larrabee's Point Orchard.

11.8 General store in Shoreham.

11.9 Junction with Route 22A; turn right, heading south.

12.4 Make left onto hard-surface road (first paved left off Route 22A).

14.7 Turn right immediately before bridge.

15.4 Road surface turns to dirt, road forks. Bear left.

16.3 Road surface returns to asphalt.

19.9 Junction with Route 73; turn right, heading west.

20.0 Back to parking area.

---

most prosperous farmlands. This is the Champlain Valley, where dairy farming is still a dominant way of life. At about 5 miles, begin to see views of Lake Champlain to the left. Reach the intersection with Route 74 at 6.1 miles. Make a left to get to Larrabee's Point, where the road ends and you have the option of a ferry ride to New York.

The side trip to Fort Ticonderoga is highly recommended. The ferry ride is short (six minutes), and it's about 1 mile from the ferry landing to the fort. Fort Ticonderoga, which has a long and colorful history, is now privately owned and carefully re-

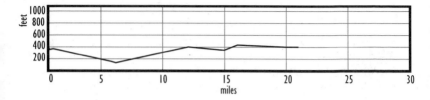

stored. A trip across the lake and up the drive to the fort provides a rare opportunity to see and feel the historical significance of this area.

Even if you don't wish to cross the lake, plan to stop at Larrabee's Point. A ferry crossing has been here since 1759, and forts have been built on both sides of the lake. In 1775, Ethan Allen crossed the lake just north of this spot on his way to capture Fort Ticonderoga. In what was the first offensive action of the American Revolution, he demanded the British surrender, "In the name of the Great Jehovah and the Continental Congress."

For those more interested in rocks than history, a few minutes of walking north along the shoreline will be rewarded with as many fossils as you can carry. Be conservative—there's still some pedaling ahead.

Backtrack on Route 74, passing the junction with Route 73, and continuing east. At 7.9 miles, pass Larrabee's Point Orchard, a handy stop during apple season. Route 74 makes some turns, and several dirt roads join it; you won't go astray if you stay on the asphalt road. At 11.8 miles you come to the town of Shoreham. You may want to refuel at the general store on the left.

Route 22A is one of Vermont's major roads and carries too much traffic to be recommended for much biking. You'll make a right onto 22A, heading south, but will only stay on it for .5 mile. At 12.4 miles, leave 22A, taking the first paved left. At 14.7 miles, just before a bridge over the outlet of Richville Pond, make a right and climb a short steep hill. At 15.4 miles, the road surface turns to hard packed dirt and the road forks. Bear left. The dirt surface returns to asphalt at 16.3 miles.

The views for the next few miles are superb. Those are the Green Mountains to your left, and the Adirondacks to your right. Cars are rare, the road is straight, and it's easy pedaling. Relax and enjoy the sweeping vistas unique to this part of the state. Again, there will be a few intersections with dirt roads; continue straight on the asphalt. At 19.9 miles, you're back in Orwell, at the intersection with Route 73. Make a right, and return to the green in front of the school.

Middlebury/Weybridge
The Otter Creek Tour

Number of Miles:	16.7
Approximate Pedaling Time:	2 hours
Terrain:	Gently rolling
Traffic:	Light
Things to See:	Shops and museums in Middlebury, Middlebury College campus, Pulp Mill Covered Bridge, University of Vermont's Morgan Horse Farm, waterfalls
Food:	Restaurants, stores in Middlebury

Otter Creek is at the center of this ride. Once known as "the Indian Road," it's the longest river in Vermont and was a major south-north travel route for Indians, and for colonists, too, when roads were little more than muddy paths. Its floodplain forms the rich farmland you'll pass through on this ride, where farmers still find Indian artifacts. Otter Creek floods regularly in the spring, occasionally forcing the closing of nearby roads. It's wise to call ahead if planning this trip in April to be sure all roads are open (802–388–4919 for state police in Middlebury).

The Pulp Mill Covered Bridge at .7 mile is thought to be one of the oldest covered bridges in Vermont. It's unusual in being a two-lane bridge of three spans, one of only two such bridges in the United States in regular use. You'll bear right after the bridge and will want to stop to look at the falls—the first of three waterfalls on this trip.

The University of Vermont's Morgan Horse Farm is at 2.0 miles. It's dedicated to breeding, training, and selling the descen-

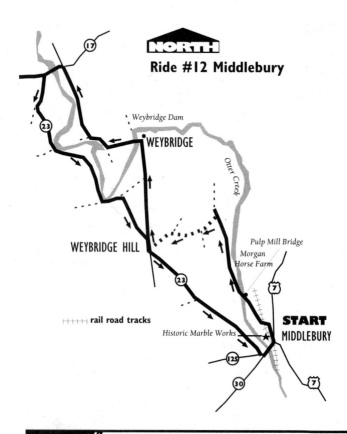

Ride #12 Middlebury

NORTH

Weybridge Dam

WEYBRIDGE

Otter Creek

WEYBRIDGE HILL

Pulp Mill Bridge
Morgan
Horse Farm

┤┤┤┤┤ **rail road tracks**

Historic Marble Works

START
MIDDLEBURY

DIRECTIONS at a glance

0.0 Parking area near train station at Historic Marble Works. Exit parking area onto Maple Street.

0.1 Stop sign. Make left onto Seymour Street, heading north.

0.7 Pulp Mill Covered Bridge.

0.8 Road forks. Bear right, following signs for Morgan Horse Farm.

2.0 University of Vermont Morgan Horse Farm on right.

2.6 Turn left onto hard packed dirt road (first left after Morgan Horse Farm).

3.0 Dirt road joins from left, continue straight.

3.5 Dirt road joins from right, continue straight.

4.0 Stop sign. Village of Weybridge Hill. Make right onto Hamilton Road, and another immediate right onto Route 23 north.

4.1 Road forks. Bear right, leaving Route 23, and following signs for Weybridge.

5.9 Enter village of Weybridge.

6.0 Road makes sharp left and crosses Otter Creek at Weybridge Dam.

8.3 Intersection with Route 17. Make left onto Route 17 west.

8.5 Cross bridge over Otter Creek.

8.7 Turn left off Route 17 onto Route 23 south, following signs for Middlebury.

12.4 Begin climb to Weybridge Hill.

13.3 Intersection in Weybridge Hill. Bear right, then left, following signs for Route 23 south.

14.6 Begin to see views of Middlebury College campus ahead to right.

15.4 Entering residential areas on outskirts of Middlebury.

16.2 Stop sign. Make left onto Route 125.

16.3 Junction with Route 30. Bear left onto Route 30 (Main Street).

16.4 Turn left off Main Street onto Mill Street.
16.5 Stop and walk bike across footbridge over Otter Creek.
16.7 Return to Marble Works parking lot.

---

dants of the stallion Justin Morgan received in payment for a debt in 1790.

At 2.6 miles, make a left onto a dirt road. If you have skinny tires, you may have to slow down a bit, but it won't be a great hardship. Most dirt roads in this part of the state are hard packed, and well maintained. A couple of other dirt roads join this one between here and Weybridge Hill. Just continue straight, enjoying views of the Adirondacks ahead and Green Mountains behind.

Come to a stop at 4.0 miles in the tiny village of Weybridge Hill. Visitors frequently remark that Vermont seems to have at least two or three, often more, towns with essentially the same name (Weybridge, Weybridge Hill, Middlebury, East Middlebury). It can be a source of confusion, particularly as locals often seem to have their own versions as well as the official designations!

Stop on the bridge over Otter Creek in Weybridge (5.9 miles) to look at the Weybridge Dam. During spring runoff, spray from the falls covers the road. For the next few miles you'll be following Otter Creek as it winds its way north. It's beautiful farmland and easy pedaling, both heading north and returning south on Route 23.

Accounts of early explorers and settlers describe Otter Creek's abundant fish and wildlife, including beaver and otters (hence the name). Although not as plentiful as they once were, otters are still seen. Even if you're not lucky enough to spot an otter, you might see an "otter slide" (path where they've enjoyed sliding into the water) on a muddy bank.

At about 12.4 miles, begin the only real climb of the trip.

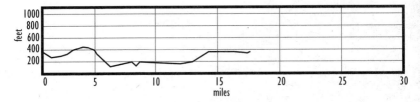

Now you'll know why that village is called Weybridge *Hill.* You'll recognize the intersection at 13.3 miles, but this time you'll stay on Route 23, heading south. A couple more miles of gently rolling hills, and you're back in Middlebury.

In Middlebury, watch carefully for the left off Main Street onto Mill Street (more like an alley). Less than .1 mile down Mill Street there is a footbridge over Otter Creek, on your right. The footbridge and park on the other side are recent additions, designed to offer a splendid view of Middlebury Falls. Walk your bike over the footbridge, and you're back in the Marble Works. If time permits, plan to visit some of Middlebury's shops and museums. Otter Creek Brewery on Exchange Street and the Frog Hollow Craft Center are examples of fun places to tour.

Dead Creek/Chimney Point

A Waterfowl Tour

Number of Miles:	16.8
Approximate Pedaling Time:	1¾ hours
Terrain:	Flat
Traffic:	Light to moderate
Things to See:	Dead Creek Wildlife Area, waterfowl, especially migrating geese in autumn, Chimney Point State Historic Site and Museum, views of Lake Champlain and the Adirondacks
Food:	West Addison Country Store at 3.7 miles, Bridge Family Restaurant near museum
Facilities:	Chimney Point Museum

This is about as flat as a Vermont bike ride can get. Pick a high gear as you start, and if you wish, leave it there for the entire ride. It's a beautiful trip any time of year but is especially recommended for fall, during the waterfowl migration. Canada geese regularly stop here, and in recent years, large flocks of snow geese have adopted the Dead Creek area as a resting point in their migration from the eastern arctic to the southern states. The parking area where the ride begins is part of the Dead Creek Wildlife Management Area. In October, the peak of the migration, you'll find yourself in the company of lots of bird watchers. Canada geese tend to arrive earlier in the month, snow geese a little later. If seeing the geese is a goal (and it's a very impressive sight), plan to start the ride early in the morning or later in the

NORTH

Ride #13 Dead Creek

*Dead Creek
Waterfowl Area*

17

★ **START**

Lake St.

17

Lake Champlain

17

WEST
ADDISON

DAR State Park

Jersey St.

New York

Vermont

Chimney Point Museum

125

*McCuen Slang
Waterfowl Area*

Basin Harbor Rd.

125

Lake St.

125

HOW *to get there* From the Burlington area, take Route 7 south to the intersection with Route 22A, just north of Vergennes. Turn right onto Route 22A and proceed about 7 miles to the intersection with Route 17. Turn right onto Route 17 and take it west 2.2 miles to a large parking area on the right, the Dead Creek Wildlife Area Access. Park here.

DIREC-TIONS at a glance

0.0 Turn right out of parking area at Dead Creek Wildlife Area onto Route 17, heading west.

0.1 Cross bridge over Dead Creek.

1.5 Road forks. Bear left, continuing on Route 17. Enter town of West Addison.

2.4 Hard surface road to the left. Continue straight on Route 17.

3.6 Road forks. Bear left, continuing on Route 17. West Addison Country Store on the right.

3.7 Hard surface road to the right. Continue on Route 17.

4.5 DAR State Park on right.

5.4 Cross bridge over Hospital Creek.

5.8 Road forks. Bear right to make short side trip to Chimney Point State Historic Site.

5.9 Turn left at museum entrance, proceed up drive to museum building.

6.0 Retrace your route to intersection of Routes 17 and 125.

6.1 Bear right onto Route 125, heading south along the lake.

7.6 McCuen Slang Waterfowl Area on the right.

9.1 Hard surface road to the right. Continue on Route 125.

9.6 Turn left off Route 125 onto Basin Harbor Road.

11.0 Town Line Road (dirt) crosses. Basin Harbor Road now called Jersey Street. Continue straight.

14.2 Town of West Addison. Church on left. Hard surface road to the left. Continue straight.

14.4 Junction with Route 17. Turn right onto Route 17, heading east.

15.2 Road forks. Bear right, continuing on Route 17.

16.7 Cross bridge over Dead Creek.

16.8 Turn left off Route 17, returning to parking area.

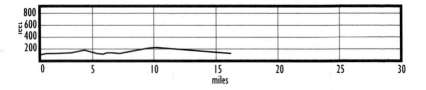

afternoon when they're likely to be feeding and moving from field to field. Winds off the lake can be cold. If you plan a fall trip, bring extra clothing.

The ride starts by heading west toward Lake Champlain. Views of the Adirondacks directly ahead can be spectacular. This is the Lake Champlain Valley, characterized by flat fertile farmlands, corn fields and cows, and long vistas in all directions. At about 3.7 miles, Route 17 swings south, and you'll soon start to notice that Lake Champlain is directly to your right. The DAR State Park is on the right at 4.5 miles (minimal day use fee). The shoreline here is rocky. Although there is no official beach at the park, people swim off the rocky shore. The limestones along the lake are also good fossil-hunting territory. At 5.4 miles, cross Hospital Creek, so named because the British set up a hospital here during the French and Indian Wars.

The route includes a very short side trip to the Chimney Point State Historic Site, adjacent to the Lake Champlain Bridge. It's a fine little museum, which houses displays on the history of the area from prehistoric through modern times. Even those who don't care to visit the museum are likely to enjoy a stop to admire the views of the lake and Crown Point on the opposite shore. Like Ticonderoga to the south, this area was considered a strategic stronghold during the colonial and Revolutionary periods. The ruins of the forts at Crown Point are directly across the lake, just north of the bridge.

After the side trip to Chimney Point, the route continues southward along the lake shore. Route 125 is close to the lake, and there are a number of handy pull-offs. The McCuen Slang

Waterfowl Area, at 7.6 miles, is another place to look for geese, ducks, and herons.

At 9.6 miles, make a left onto Basin Harbor Road. (That's what it's called here. Its name will change to Jersey Street as you cross the town line.) Traffic will be very sparse now, the road surface is good, and views of the Adirondacks to the left will be lovely, with occasional glimpses of the lake. You can't help but notice the dairy farms here—you'll literally be pedaling through them as you head back to the parking area. These are family farms on a much larger, flatter scale than the hillside farms in the central part of the state. Count the silos and note the size of the herds. Many smaller Vermont farms have failed in recent years, and it's heartening to see that those in the Champlain Valley seem to be prospering.

Bristol/Starksboro
Circling the Hogback Range

Number of Miles:	23.1
Approximate Pedaling Time:	3 hours
Terrain:	Gently rolling
Traffic:	Light to moderate
Things to See:	Town of Bristol, Lord's Prayer Rock, views of Hogback Range, villages of Starksboro and Monkton Ridge
Food:	Stores and restaurants in Bristol, general stores in Starksboro and Monkton Ridge

The high peaks a few miles to the east of Bristol and Starksboro might suggest that this is a trip for hill climbers only. Not so. Considering its proximity to the spine of the Green Mountains, this route is remarkably flat. There are some hills, but they're gentle enough to make this trip seem an easy 23 miles.

For the first mile, Route 116 parallels the New Haven River. The road is narrow and twisting here and carries both north-bound and eastbound traffic. Exercise caution. Take a few moments to notice the Lord's Prayer Rock on the right at .6 miles. There are various accounts of Dr. S. Greene's reason for having the prayer chiseled in stone at this spot. According to one version, when Greene was a boy, his job was to take loads of logs from the mountaintop in South Starksboro to the sawmill in Bristol. It was a hazardous trip on a steep winding road with a number of narrow bridges. When he finally arrived at the "Big Rock," Greene knew he'd made it safely and said a little prayer of relief. Many years later, after a trip to Egypt where he saw hi-

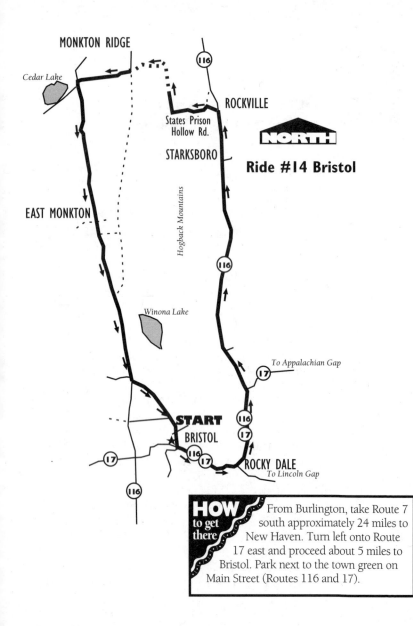

MONKTON RIDGE

Cedar Lake

116

ROCKVILLE

States Prison
Hollow Rd.

STARKSBORO

NORTH

Ride #14 Bristol

EAST MONKTON

Hogback Mountains

116

Winona Lake

To Appalachian Gap

17

START

116

BRISTOL

17

17

116

17

ROCKY DALE

To Lincoln Gap

116

HOW
to get
there
From Burlington, take Route 7
south approximately 24 miles to
New Haven. Turn left onto Route
17 east and proceed about 5 miles to
Bristol. Park next to the town green on
Main Street (Routes 116 and 17).

DIREC-TIONS at a glance

0.0	Traffic light at four-way intersection on Bristol's Main Street, at corner of town green. Proceed east on Main Street (Route 116/17).
0.6	Lord's Prayer Rock on right.
1.5	Rocky Dale. Hard-surface road on right. Continue straight on Route 116/17.
3.3	Route 17 turns right. Continue straight on Route 116.
8.6	Starksboro Country Store on left.
9.8	Turn left off Route 116 onto States Prison Hollow Road (unmarked here). This is the first paved left after Starksboro.
11.4	Road surface turns to dirt.
12.8	Road surface returns to asphalt.
12.9	Four-way intersection. Continue straight.
14.2	Village of Monkton Ridge. Road forks. Bear left. Come to stop sign. Bear left. Road immediately forks again. Bear left, following signs for Bristol.
19.4	Dirt road to left, state access area on Winona Lake.
21.0	Hard-surface road to right. Continue straight.
21.1	Road forks. Bear left.
22.7	Entering residential area of Bristol. Continue straight.
23.1	Intersection with Main Street (Route 116/17) in Bristol. Parking area to right.

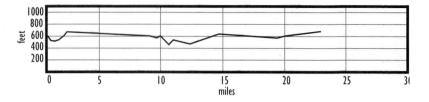

eroglyphics, he commissioned Bristol's own message in stone for travelers on a twisting road.

In Rocky Dale, at 1.4 miles, Route 116 begins to swing north. The high peaks of the Green Mountains directly east of here are a formidable barrier between eastern and western sections of the state. We're certainly not crossing them today, but you will pass by the roads to two gaps in the Green Mountains. The first is the paved road to the right in Rocky Dale, at 1.5 miles, which crosses Lincoln Gap—but is passable only in the spring, summer, and fall. The second is where Route 17 leaves Route 116, at 3.3 miles, and crosses the Appalachian Gap. That road is open all year, but it can be a hair-raising trip in winter. Neither gap is really much of a "gap" (both are more than 2,300 feet at the top). By contrast, our route (Route 116 north) is amazingly flat. It's straight and although there is a moderate amount of traffic, the shoulders are very wide. Route 116 runs the length of the beautiful valley between the main ridge of the Green Mountains to the east and the Hogback Mountains, a small subrange of the Greens, to the west. In fact, our route circles the Hogback Range.

The Starksboro Country Store is a good place for a break. Then watch carefully for the left turn off Route 116. It will be the first paved left. This is States Prison Hollow Road. There's never been a state prison here, and no one is certain about the derivation of the name. It may be that farming land as rocky as this was a lot like serving a prison sentence. Or, some think the name derives from the character of a few early residents of the area, who were thought likely candidates for serving prison time. At 11.4 miles the road surface turns to dirt for a short distance. It's generally a good hard packed surface, but folks with skinny tires should be careful of loose gravel at about 12.5 miles, where the road makes a sharp left and descends a short steep hill.

After making the left in Monkton Ridge, begin returning southward. Now you'll have views of the western slopes of the Hogback Range. This stretch of road is a bit hillier than Route 116, but it is still, for central Vermont, unusually flat. More fine views of farms, fields, and lakes end with a short climb back to Bristol.

Vergennes/Lake Champlain Maritime Museum
A Lake Champlain History Tour

Number of Miles:	14.8
Approximate Pedaling Time:	1½ hours, longer with museum or beach stop
Terrain:	Flat
Traffic:	Sparse
Things to See:	Vergennes Falls, views of Adirondack and Green Mountains, Lake Champlain, Lake Champlain Maritime Museum, Button Bay State Park, waterfowl on Dead Creek
Food:	Restaurants and stores in Vergennes, restaurant at Basin Harbor Club, general store in Panton
Facilities:	Lake Champlain Maritime Museum

Many of Vermont's most prosperous farms are in the Champlain Basin, where the soil is fertile and the land is nearly flat. If you've been riding in other parts of the state, you'll be impressed by the scale of the farms here (they're much bigger than Vermont's hillside farms). And you'll be amazed at how flat the terrain is. This is an opportunity to knock the dirt off some of those high hears, which may not get a lot of use elsewhere in Vermont. The Maritime Museum along Lake Champlain is a rare find. Riders with an interest in Revolutionary history, underwa-

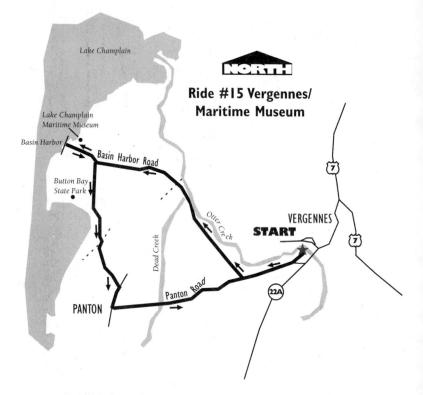

Ride #15 Vergennes/ Maritime Museum

Lake Champlain

Lake Champlain Maritime Museum

Basin Harbor

Basin Harbor Road

Button Bay State Park

Otter Creek

Dead Creek

VERGENNES

START

Panton Road

PANTON

22A

7

7

HOW to get there From Burlington, take Route 7 south about 20 miles to the intersection with Route 22A. Turn right onto Route 22A and proceed about 1 mile south into the city of Vergennes. In Vergennes, make the first right after the bridge over Otter Creek. (The road to the right, which is unmarked, goes under an overpass connecting two buildings.) Keep bearing right, following signs for Vergennes Falls Park. Park in the parking area at Vergennes Falls Park. (In spring the park may be flooded. Use parking areas next to the town green in Vergennes as an alternative.)

0.0   Parking area at Vergennes Falls Park.

0.1   Stop sign. Go left, then make an immediate right.

0.3   Stop sign. Make right, passing B. F. Goodrich Aerospace plant on the right.

1.6   Turn right onto Basin Harbor Road.

3.6   Otter Creek very close to road on the right.

3.9   Cross bridge over Dead Creek.

4.2   Webster Road (hard-surface) to left. Bear right, continuing on Basin Harbor Road.

6.0   Junction with another hard surface road. Turn right, following signs for Basin Harbor.

6.3   Mile Point Road (hard-surface) to right. Continue on Basin Harbor Road.

6.4   Entrance to Lake Champlain Maritime Museum on right.

6.4   Turn left out of Maritime Museum.

6.6   Mile Point Road to left (hard-surface). Continue on Basin Harbor Road.

6.9   Road forks. Bear right on Button Bay Road.

7.7   Entrance to Button Bay State Park

8.0   Button Bay Boat Access Area on right.

9.8   Hard-surface road joins from the left. Continue straight on Button Bay Road.

10.2   Village of Panton. General store on right. Turn left onto Panton Road and begin heading east.

11.3   Bridge over Dead Creek.

13.1   Basin Harbor Road to left. (Have now completed a loop.) Continue straight.

14.4   Pass B. F. Goodrich Aerospace plant on left, make a left turn onto hard-surface road.

14.6   Bear left, then make an immediate right to return to Vergennes Falls Park.

14.8   Back to parking area.

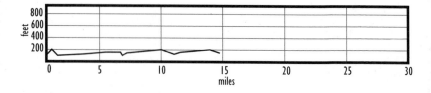

ter archeology, boat construction, or the ecology of the lake will want to plan an extended stop.

The trip's starting point is at a picturesque spot below the Vergennes Falls. Signs tell you that this is the end of the canoe portage around the falls for paddlers on Otter Creek. This parking area floods regularly during high water in the spring. During April, you may need to use an alternative parking spot on the green in Vergennes. For much of the early part of the trip, Otter Creek is close to the road, on the right. The stretch of road at about 3.6 miles is a popular fishing area. Pay attention to where you walk if you decide to take a break along here: The poison ivy looks very healthy.

Dramatic views of the Adirondacks begin at about 0.8 miles, and continue for much of the trip. After bearing right at 6.0 miles, the Adirondacks will briefly be to your left and the Green Mountains to your right. Camel's Hump is the most prominent of the Green Mountain peaks seen from here. Samuel de Champlain first called it *le lion couchant*—the couching, or resting, lion. It does look more like a sphinx than a camel.

The Lake Champlain Maritime Museum (6.4 miles) is a good resting point. It's privately owned and has an official policy of being bicycle friendly. Cyclists are welcome to use the picnic areas, water fountain, and rest rooms, even if not visiting the museum. And many will decide to visit (moderate admission fee). Collections include displays of old boats—from Indian dugouts to ice boats—chronicles of ongoing underwater archeological projects, a floating replica of the *Philadelphia* (one of Benedict Arnold's gunboats, which fought the British at Valcour

Island), boat-building demonstrations, and more.

Our route has riders backtrack after the museum stop. However, continuing past the museum for a short distance (quarter mile or less) takes you on a side trip to Basin Harbor, a resort community with golf course and restaurant, as well as a beautiful view of the tiny harbor.

Button Bay State Park (7.7 miles) is another good stopping point (nominal admission fee). It offers swimming (pool or lake), picnicking, and fossil hunting along the rocky shore. You may see chunks of fossilized coral reef, fossil sea snails, or the oddly shaped stones, which look a bit like buttons, formed by water percolating through the clay soil of the area (hence "Button Bay").

At 10.2 miles, begin heading east and back toward Vergennes. In another mile, as you cross the bridge over Dead Creek, take a few moments to look for waterfowl and wading birds. Herons are common, and in the fall this area is an important stop for geese migrating along the Champlain flyway.

Ascutney
Round the Monadnock

Number of Miles:	23.3
Approximate Pedaling Time:	3 hours
Terrain:	One steep climb, otherwise rolling or long downhill
Traffic:	Moderate (Routes 131 and 5) to light (Routes 106, 44, and 44A)
Things to See:	Views of Mt. Ascutney from all angles, Indian Stones near Knapp Brook, towns of Reading and Brownsville, Ascutney State Park
Food:	General stores in Downers, Reading, and Brownsville
Facilities:	General store in Downers, Ascutney State Park

Mt. Ascutney is a monadnock. Geologists explain that a monadnock is a mass of bedrock (granite here) that is more durable than its surroundings and so has better resisted erosion than the land around it. Unlike the Green Mountains, which are a range of peaks, Mt. Ascutney stands essentially alone. This ride circles Ascutney, so you'll get a chance to study it from all angles.

The first 3.5 miles of the trip, westward on Route 131, are uphill. Signs from the other direction warn trucks of an 8 percent grade. Although that's not incredibly steep, you'll know you've done some climbing. Traffic can be significant on Route 131. There is a level shoulder, although it isn't terribly wide. Stay right, and stay alert. That's Mt. Ascutney to your right, and this is your chance to study its southern slopes. Trucks are also

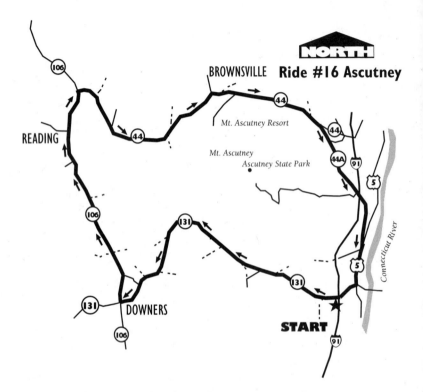

NORTH

BROWNSVILLE **Ride #16 Ascutney**

READING

Mt. Ascutney Resort

Mt. Ascutney
Ascutney State Park

Connecticut River

DOWNERS

START

HOW *to get there* — From the Brattleboro area, take I–91 north to exit 8. At the end of the exit ramp, turn left onto Route 131 west. Pass under I–91 and make an immediate left into the Park and Ride parking area. The ride begins from here.

DIREC-TIONS at a glance

0.0 Turn left out of the Park and Ride area off Interstate 91 onto Route 131, heading west. Begin ascent.

0.7 Begin views of Mt. Ascutney to the right.

3.5 Reach crest of hill. Start descent.

6.7 Stop sign at intersection with Route 106. Downers Corner Store on opposite corner. Turn right onto Route 106 north.

10.2 Historic marker on right for Indian Stones.

10.9 Town of Reading. Reading Country Store on left.

11.8 Turn right off Route 106 onto Route 44 east, following signs for Ascutney Mountain Resort.

11.9 Cross Mill Brook.

14.2 Unusual covered bridge on dirt road to right. Continue straight on Route 44.

16.0 Town of Brownsville.

16.2 Brownsville General Store on right.

16.7 Entrance to Ascutney Mountain Resort. Continue straight on Route 44.

18.7 Road forks. Bear right onto Route 44A south, following signs for Ascutney.

19.2 Paved road to the left. Continue straight on Route 44A.

20.5 Entrance to Mt. Ascutney State Park on right.

20.7 Cross bridge over I–91.

21.6 Stop sign at junction with Route 5. Turn right onto Route 5 south.

22.7 Turn right off Route 5 onto Route 131 west.

23.2 Pass under I–91.

23.3 Turn left off Route 131 into Park and Ride parking area.

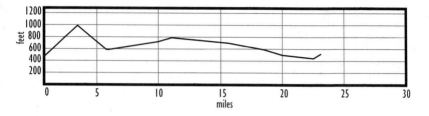

warned of an 8 percent grade going down the other side of this hill. You'll find that the stretch from 3.5 to 6.7 miles (from the crest to the intersection with Route 106) goes by quickly. Be especially careful during the final mile of this downhill, where turns are tight and visibility is poor.

The Downers Corner Store, at the intersection of Routes 131 and 106, is a friendly stop. It has a sign out front welcoming trucks, buses, and bikers and announcing that a rest room is available. Route 106 is a nice biking road, and this stretch feels unusually flat. In reality, you'll be very gradually, almost imperceptibly, going uphill. The North Branch of the Black River will be to your right along Route 106. Note that you're following it upstream. And now, at least for part of this stretch, you'll have views of Ascutney's western slopes.

On the right at 10.2 miles is an interesting historical marker. This marks not a battlefield or a historic building, but the site of a minor event in Vermont's history: the birth of a baby to James and Susanna Johnson, captives of Abnaki Indians en route to Montreal. It's a commemoration that helps us see colonial history from the perspective of the European people who settled and farmed and struggled in this area. It's gratifying to know that sites like this, as well as the battlefields and the buildings, are on the National Register of Historic Places.

After the right turn onto Route 44, you'll be doing a lot of gradual coasting: You're following Mill Brook as it heads toward the Connecticut River. As you progress along Route 44, you'll have fine views of Ascutney's northern slopes. At 16.7 miles, in the middle of a short climb, is the entrance to the Ascutney Mountain Resort—Ascutney's ski area. You'll probably already have noticed the ski trails on the mountain. Note that the ski area is on the northern side of the mountain, where snow melts more slowly.

Watch for the turn, at 18.7 miles, onto Route 44A. Virtually the entire stretch of Route 44A is downhill. The entrance to Mt. Ascutney State Park is on the right at 20.5 miles. Serious bikers like to race up the road to the summit (an increase of more than 2,300 feet in elevation). That side trip is a bit outside the scope of this collection, but a wonderful view is guaranteed to those who attempt it (nominal admission fee).

The downhill ends at 21.6 miles, at the junction with Route 5. More traffic on Route 5 necessitates greater care. The intersection of Routes 5 and 131, at 22.7 miles looks congested, but the road is wide enough to accommodate traffic going to the interstate. Just stay right, obey traffic regulations, and you're back to the Park and Ride area in short order.

Windsor Bridge
The Longest in the World

Number of Miles: 11.5
Approximate Pedaling Time: 1½ hours
Terrain: Flat
Traffic: Moderate
Things to See: Cornish-Windsor Covered Bridge, Connecticut River, town of Windsor, American Precision Museum, Old Constitution House, views of Mt. Ascutney
Food: Stores and restaurants in Windsor

It's hard to pass up an opportunity to pedal across the longest wooden bridge in the United States. The Cornish-Windsor Covered Bridge is the centerpiece of this ride, and a very impressive centerpiece it is. The ride as a whole is very flat and not quite as scenic as its proximity to the Connecticut River might suggest. The two Connecticut River crossings, however, are an experience to remember. You'll want to bring your camera on this one.

The first 5 miles, from the Weathersfield town offices to Windsor along Route 5, are less than delightful. In spite of the nearby interstate, Route 5 has a fair amount of traffic. Its shoulders vary from narrow to quite adequate. Although the map assures us that the Connecticut River is immediately to the right, views of it are generally obstructed. But it's a fast 5 miles, and though not delightful, it's not unpleasant.

There are a couple of possible stops in Windsor. The first is the American Precision Museum, on the left at 4.7 miles. It houses an astounding collection of machine tools, from sewing

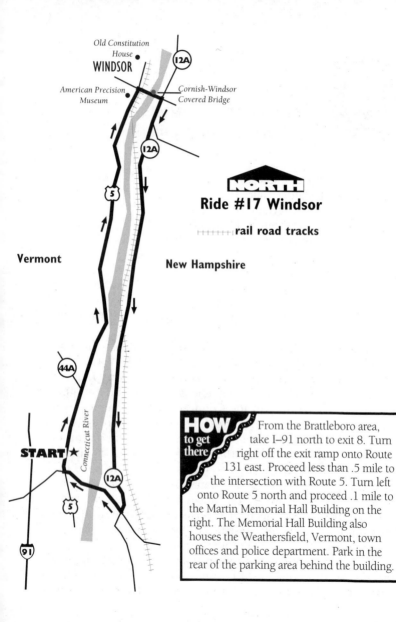

Old Constitution House

WINDSOR

American Precision Museum

Cornish-Windsor Covered Bridge

12A

12A

5

NORTH

Ride #17 Windsor

┼┼┼┼┼┼ **rail road tracks**

Vermont

New Hampshire

44A

Connecticut River

START ★

12A

5

91

HOW to get there From the Brattleboro area, take I–91 north to exit 8. Turn right off the exit ramp onto Route 131 east. Proceed less than .5 mile to the intersection with Route 5. Turn left onto Route 5 north and proceed .1 mile to the Martin Memorial Hall Building on the right. The Memorial Hall Building also houses the Weathersfield, Vermont, town offices and police department. Park in the rear of the parking area behind the building.

DIRECTIONS at a glance

0.0 Turn right out of the driveway for the Weathersfield town offices onto Route 5, heading north.

1.0 Junction with Route 44A on left. Continue straight on Route 5.

4.7 American Precision Museum on left.

4.8 Traffic light and four-way intersection. Turn right off Route 5 onto Bridge Street.

5.0 Enter Cornish-Windsor Covered Bridge.

5.1 Exit Cornish-Windsor Covered Bridge. Turn right onto New Hampshire Route 12A.

5.5 Road forks. Bear right, continuing on Route 12A south.

6.4 Historic marker at Chase House on left.

8.1 Cross railroad track.

10.1 Paved road to the right. Continue straight on Route 12A.

10.5 Traffic light and four-way intersection. Turn right off Route 12A, following signs for Ascutney, Vermont.

11.0 Cross bridge over Connecticut River.

11.4 Traffic light and four-way intersection. Turn right onto Route 5 north. (Use short sidewalk/bikepath next to road.)

11.5 Turn right off Route 5 into driveway for parking area for Weathersfield town offices.

---

machines to lathes. Even those who aren't particularly mechanically inclined will find items of interest. The second stop is a short side trip to the Old Constitution House. (Instead of turning onto Bridge Street, continue straight on Route 5 for less than .5 mile. It's on the left.) This is the former tavern where, in 1777, the Vermont constitution was drafted and adopted. Vermont was to remain an independent republic for fourteen years before becoming the fourteenth state in 1791. Ever independently minded, the Vermonters incorporated into their constitu-

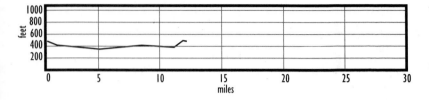

tion ideas that had never before been included in the written foundation of a government. Most notably, slavery was prohibited, and every man older than twenty-one who had lived in the state for a year was guaranteed the right to vote. It's a modest little museum but the site of some grand plans.

At 5.0 miles, cross the Cornish-Windsor Covered Bridge, longest wooden bridge in the United States and longest two-span covered bridge in the world. The inside is artificially lighted, but do remove your sun glasses. It's a two-lane bridge, but it doesn't have much extra space beside the lanes. Bikers are advised to wait until the bridge is empty before crossing. Immediately to the right on the New Hampshire side is a handy pull-off and historic marker, which describes the bridge's construction and history. This is also a spot with a lovely view of the river—a definite photo opportunity.

Route 12A, along the New Hampshire side of the river, is a fine biking road. Although views of the river are again generally obstructed, views of Mt. Ascutney in Vermont are excellent. Another photo opportunity comes along at around 10.0 miles as you pass Ascutney View Farm. You'll agree the farm is well named.

A final—and perhaps the best—opportunity for picture taking comes as you cross the bridge from New Hampshire back into Vermont. The bridge is only two lanes, but it has an enormous shoulder, the size at least of another lane, on each side. It's possible and even quite comfortable to stop in the middle of the bridge to admire the river.

Plymouth
The Coolidge Triangle

Number of Miles:	18.1
Approximate Pedaling Time:	2 hours
Terrain:	Moderate hills with one short steep ascent and one long gradual descent
Traffic:	Moderate
Things to See:	Calvin Coolidge Birthplace and Homestead, village of Plymouth Notch, Long Trail Brewing Company, Ottauquechee River
Food:	General store in Plymouth Notch
Facilities:	Visitor center at Coolidge Historical Site

This triangular circuit is one of the stages of the Killington Stage Race, a bike race that is quickly becoming one of the nation's premier cycling events. For their first day, the pro racers do the Plymouth circuit six times, averaging just a little more than forty minutes per circuit. Casual pedalers will want to plan for longer than forty minutes (maybe a lot longer) for the trip. It's not just that the racers pedal faster than most of the rest of us; they don't stop to enjoy the sights.

Route 100, the first leg of our triangle, offers some climbing, some coasting, and some wonderful scenery: hemlock forests, Woodward Reservoir, and mountain streams where people pan for gold. However, Route 100 carries more than the ideal amount of traffic. Stay right, and stay alert.

Turn left at 5.2 miles onto the second leg of the triangle and start uphill. The first .4 mile are the steepest. Some riders will

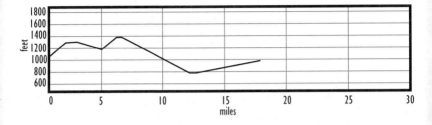

want to take a break from pedaling and walk the bike up part of this hill. The entrance to the Coolidge Birthplace and Homestead in Plymouth Notch (6.2 miles) is just past the highest elevation on the route. This historic site is definitely worth a stop. A modest admission fee gains entrance to a number of buildings. The house where Coolidge was born and the house across the street where his father administered the presidential oath of office remain unchanged. Plymouth Notch is a typical little Vermont village and a nice stop even if you don't have time for the historic sights. Coolidge was clearly thinking of home when he said, "I love Vermont because of her hills and valleys, her scenery and invigorating climate, but most of all because of her indomitable people." The rest of the Route 100A leg of the trip is a lovely long downhill (6 miles of descent).

The third leg of the triangle, from Bridgewater Corners to West Bridgewater, is one of the very few sections of Route 4 that can be considered safe for bikers. Traffic is heavy, but the road is straight, and it has enormous paved shoulders. Immediately after the turn onto Route 4, pass the Long Trail Brewing Company on the left. (Their visitor center has windows on the brewing and bottling area, and they sell samples.) It's uphill now to the end of the ride, but a very gradual, even comfortable, uphill. Route 4 crisscrosses the Ottauquechee River several times between Bridgewater Corners and West Bridgewater. It's thought that the river's name is from a Natick Indian word for "swift mountain stream." In the spring or after a heavy rain the Ot-

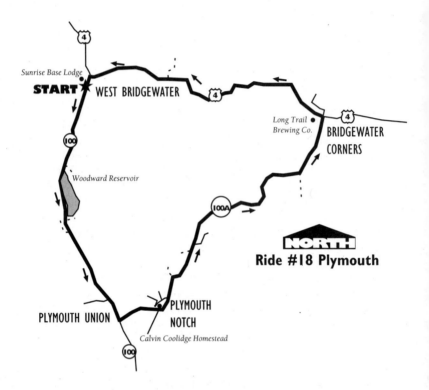

Ride #18 Plymouth

HOW to get there From Rutland, take Route 4 east about 17 miles to the intersection with Route 100 south. Turn right onto Route 100 south and come immediately to Killington Ski Area's Sunrise Base Lodge on the right. Park in the large base lodge parking area.

DIREC-TIONS at a glance

0.0 Turn right out of parking area at Killington's Sunrise Base Lodge onto Route 100 south.

1.7 Begin passing Woodward Reservoir on left.

1.8 Fishing access area on Woodward Reservoir.

2.8 Southern end Woodward Reservoir.

5.2 Village of Plymouth Union. Turn left off Route 100 onto Route 100A. Begin climb.

5.6 End of steepest section of uphill to Plymouth Notch.

6.1 Hard-surface road on left to village of Plymouth Notch. Continue on Route 100A.

6.2 Parking area for Coolidge Homestead on left.

7.9 Coolidge State Park on right.

12.1 Cross Ottauquechee River.

12.2 Junction with Route 4. Turn left onto Route 4, heading west.

12.3 Long Trail Brewing Company on left.

18.0 Turn left off Route 4 onto Route 100 south.

18.1 Return to Sunrise Base Lodge parking area.

tauquechee can be a rushing torrent. On a hot summer day, it's a pleasant place to cool your feet.

Woodstock/Barnard
To Silver Lake

Number of Miles: 19
Approximate Pedaling Time: 2½ hours
Terrain: Mostly uphill first half of trip, downhill second half
Traffic: Moderate on Route 12, light elsewhere
Things to See: Billings Farm and Museum, site of first ski lift in the U.S.; town of Barnard, Silver Lake, Suicide Six Ski Area
Food: General stores in Barnard and South Pomfret
Facilities: Billings Farm and Museum

Our route begins at the parking area of the Billings Farm and Museum on the outskirts of Woodstock. Woodstock is one of the showcases of Vermont. It's known for impeccably restored Federal-style houses, a large elliptical green, and its many cultural and environmental projects. Twentieth-century restorations are largely thanks to the interest and money of Laurance Rockefeller, whose wife was the granddaughter of Frederick Billings (of Northern Pacific Railroad fame and fortune). The Rockefellers established the Billings Farm and Museum, which is dedicated to the preservation of the techniques and heritage of the nineteenth-century Vermont farm. Woodstock is an interesting side trip at the beginning or end of this ride, but be forewarned: The attractions here make for a lot of visitors and a lot of traffic.

Be sure to notice the historic marker on the right at 1.6 miles. Although it's not much of a hill by today's ski standards,

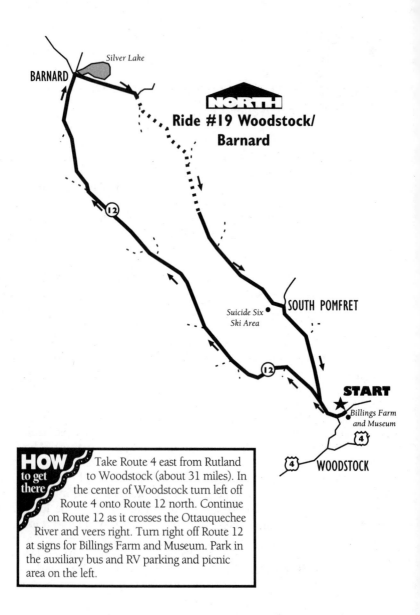

Silver Lake

BARNARD

12

NORTH

**Ride #19 Woodstock/
Barnard**

SOUTH POMFRET

Suicide Six
Ski Area

12

START

Billings Farm
and Museum

4

4 **WOODSTOCK**

**HOW
to get
there** Take Route 4 east from Rutland
to Woodstock (about 31 miles). In
the center of Woodstock turn left off
Route 4 onto Route 12 north. Continue
on Route 12 as it crosses the Ottauquechee
River and veers right. Turn right off Route 12
at signs for Billings Farm and Museum. Park in
the auxiliary bus and RV parking and picnic
area on the left.

DIREC-TIONS
at a glance

0.0 Turn right out of the Billings Farm and Museum bus and RV parking and picnic area. Make an immediate right onto Route 12 heading north.

0.6 Hard-surface road to the right. Continue straight on Route 12 north.

1.6 Historic marker on right notes site of first U.S. rope tow.

8.2 Crest of hill. Begin descent into Barnard.

9.7 Four-way intersection in town of Barnard. Turn right off Route 12 onto road that passes between Barnard General Store and Silver Lake.

10.9 Road forks. Bear right. Road surface immediately turns to dirt.

12.8 Dirt road enters from left. Continue straight.

13.4 Road surface returns to asphalt.

16.0 Suicide Six Ski Area on right.

16.2 South Pomfret General Store on left. Hard-surface road enters from left. Continue straight.

18.3 Junction with Route 12. Bear left onto Route 12 south.

18.9 Turn left off Route 12 to Billings Farm and Museum.

19.0 Return to parking area.

---

this is the birthplace of downhill skiing in America. In 1934, a rope tow powered by a Model T engine pulled skiers up the pasture hill of Clinton Gilbert's farm and set the stage for Vermont's ski industry. Near the end of this ride—really just over the hill to the east—you'll pass the Suicide Six Ski Area. Still operating and a favorite of many local families, it was one of the first commercial ski areas in the country.

It's more or less uphill from Woodstock to Barnard. Most of the ascent is fairly gradual, and there will be stretches when you'll hardly be aware of climbing. The steepest section is shortly before you reach the crest of the climb (at about 8.2

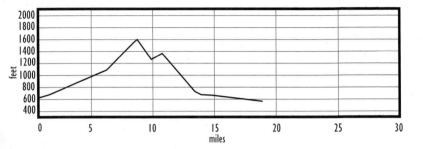

miles). Then it's a short downhill to Barnard and Silver Lake.

The general store has apparently been the center of activity in Barnard since 1832. Don't miss the classic soda fountain in the rear of the store (great root beer floats). The town picnic and swimming area across the street from the store, on Silver Lake, is a good place to relax. Like most Vermont villages, Barnard has assorted claims to fame. Sinclair Lewis was a Barnard resident when he was the first American to receive the Nobel Prize for literature. For more than a century it was believed that the last documented catamount (mountain lion) in Vermont was shot in Barnard in 1881. It seems now that it wasn't the last. There have been reports of sightings of the big cats over the years, and in 1994, experts confirmed their reappearance in the northern part of the state near Eligo Lake (see Hardwick/Greensboro ride).

Barnard residents are fond of explaining to visitors that it's all downhill from Barnard. They mean this literally—all surrounding towns are indeed at a lower elevation. Our route has you do just a little climbing, however, before you begin the long downhill back to Woodstock. Be sure to bear right when the road forks at 10.9 miles. It turns to dirt immediately after the fork and is moderately steep in spots. It remains a dirt surface for 2.5 miles, then returns to asphalt. The remainder of the trip is a gradually rolling descent, which takes you by some beautiful old farmhouses (both restored and unrestored), past the Suicide Six Ski Area, and by the South Pomfret General Store.

Quechee/Pomfret
Across the Watershed and Back

Number of Miles:	25.6
Approximate Pedaling Time:	3½ hours
Terrain:	Hilly
Traffic:	Light
Things to See:	Village of Quechee, Ottauquechee River, White River, villages of North Pomfret, Pomfret, and South Pomfret, Billings Farm and Museum, Taftsville Covered Bridge
Food:	Restaurants and stores in Quechee, general stores in North Pomfret and South Pomfret
Facilities:	Billings Farm and Museum

This ride crosses the watershed between the Ottauquechee River and the White River, and then crosses back again to the Ottauquechee. That means up, down, up, down—with lots of picture postcard scenery. If not the easiest ride in this collection, it's certainly one of the prettiest.

Quechee, our starting point, represents the upscale end of Vermont's social and economic spectrum. Formerly a small New England mill town whose woolen industry harnessed the Ottauquechee River, Quechee is now known for its expensive condo communities, golf courses, and specialty shops. One new industry has forged a link with the town's past: The Simon Pearce Glass Works, which produces handblown glassware, is located in an old mill and uses the Quechee waterfall for hydropower.

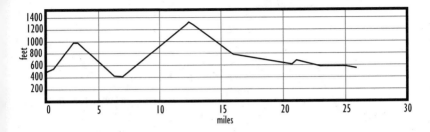

The first 2.5 miles will be gradually uphill, to the top of the watershed between the Ottauquechee and the White River. Then it's downhill to the White River. Our route parallels the White for about a mile, then heads west and begins another crossing of the watershed.

The 5-mile section from the White River to Pomfret is a long gradual uphill. Take your time. The road crosses Mill Brook several times, scenery is quintessential *Vermont Life,* and traffic is very sparse. You'll probably arrive at the North Pomfret General Store about the time your energy level has hit low. It's a good place for a break and a snack. You won't really be to the top of the watershed until you reach Pomfret, in a couple more miles. Watch for signs at about 11.0 miles: There is a hard-surface road to the right (to Sharon), which would take you back down to the White River. Continue straight, following signs for Woodstock.

At about 12.5 miles, you're at the top of the watershed and the pace will accelerate. It's time to stop admiring the scenery, to shift gears, and to concentrate on the descent to the Ottauquechee River. The first 3 miles are the steepest (steeper than the section coming up from the White River). Use caution and use your brakes. The fastest part of the descent ends in South Pomfret, at a junction with another hard-surface road. There's a general store at the corner and a town park across the road, in case it's time for another snack.

As you make a left off Route 12, at 18.4 miles, you'll pass the entrance to the Billings Farm and Museum, a working farm that

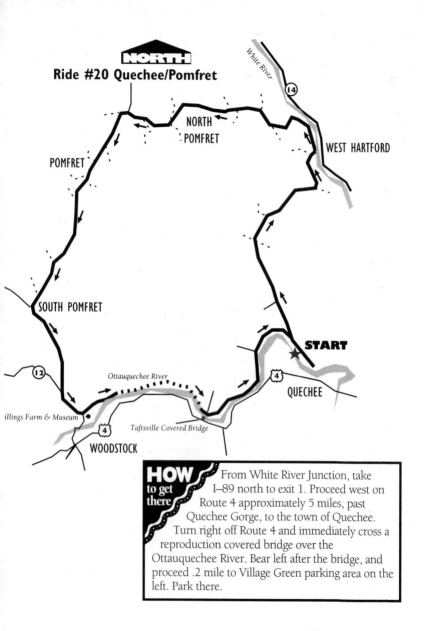

Ride #20 Quechee/Pomfret

NORTH

White River

14

NORTH
POMFRET

WEST HARTFORD

POMFRET

SOUTH POMFRET

START

12

Ottauquechee River

4

QUECHEE

illings Farm & Museum

4

Taftsville Covered Bridge

WOODSTOCK

HOW to get there From White River Junction, take I–89 north to exit 1. Proceed west on Route 4 approximately 5 miles, past Quechee Gorge, to the town of Quechee. Turn right off Route 4 and immediately cross a reproduction covered bridge over the Ottauquechee River. Bear left after the bridge, and proceed .2 mile to Village Green parking area on the left. Park there.

DIREC-TIONS at a glance

0.0	Turn left out of Village Green parking area.
0.7	Road forks. Bear right. Begin uphill.
1.6	Hard-surface road enters from left. Continue straight.
2.5	Begin downhill.
5.8	Turn left onto Pomfret Road immediately before bridge over White River.

6.8 Road swings away from river, begin uphill.

9.9 Village of North Pomfret. Post office and general store on left.

11.0 Hard-surface road enters from right. Continue straight, following signs for Woodstock.

12.5 Pomfret Center School on left, town hall on right. Begin downhill.

15.8 Stop sign at junction with another hard-surface road. Village of South Pomfret. General store on right. Turn left.

17.8 Stop sign at junction with Route 12. Turn left onto Route 12, heading south.

18.4 Turn left off Route 12 onto hard-surface road. Entrance to Billings Farm and Museum is immediately on right.

19.3 Road surface changes to dirt.

20.1 Road forks. Bear right, staying next to the river.

21.3 Road forks again. Bear right, staying next to the river.

21.5 Junction with a hard-surface road. Dam and Taftsville Covered Bridge to the right. Turn left.

21.7 Hard-surface road enters from the left. Continue straight, following the river.

23.8 Another hard-surface road enters from the left. Continue straight.

24.0 Another hard-surface road enters from the left. Continue straight.

25.6 Back to parking area.

preserves the heritage of the nineteenth-century Vermont family farm (moderate admission fee). For those interested in a side trip, the town of Woodstock (exquisitely restored homes, many stores, lots of traffic) is just ahead on Route 12.

A cautionary note: On a road map, it appears that Route 4 between Woodstock and Quechee might be a sensible alternative route. It isn't. Route 4 is VERY busy. This stretch, which is narrow, winding, and has no shoulders, is particularly dangerous. If you make a side trip to Woodstock, come back to the intersection by the Billings Farm to make the return trip to Quechee. Don't take Route 4.

The road along the north bank of the Ottauquechee turns to dirt for a couple of miles. It's a pleasant, hard packed dirt road, which won't be a problem for skinny tires. The road is very close to the river for most of this stretch of the ride. On a hot day, you'll probably see canoes, swimmers, and kids leaping from a rope swing into a swimming hole. You may want to take a few minutes to cool off too.

Thetford/Lake Fairlee
Through All the Thetfords

Number of Miles:	18.4
Approximate Pedaling Time:	2 hours
Terrain:	Rolling, with climbs at beginning and end
Traffic:	Moderate
Things to See:	Village of Thetford Hill, Lake Fairlee, views of Connecticut River, cemetery in East Thetford
Food:	General stores in Thetford Center, Post Mills, and East Thetford; Lunch Box snack bar between East Thetford and Thetford Hill
Facilities:	Treasure Island public beach on Lake Fairlee

This trip takes you through the beautiful colonial village of Thetford Hill, by summer cottages on Lake Fairlee, and down the edge of the Connecticut River, the superhighway of the region's early history. Although it wouldn't be difficult to do this ride in two hours, you may want to take longer. There's a lot to see, a place to swim, and many photo opportunities.

The first mile, to the village of Thetford Hill, is uphill and is the steepest part of the trip. By the time you get there, you'll feel that Thetford Hill is aptly named. Take time to ride or walk around the town green, which is surrounded by picturesque colonial houses. The Congregational Church (1787) is the oldest church in Vermont that has been in continuous use since construction.

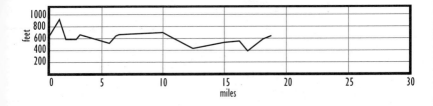

The village of Thetford Center is just 1.2 miles to the west of Thetford Hill. Thetford is one of Vermont's many towns that encompass a number of villages. You'll see Thetford Hill, Thetford Center, North Thetford, and East Thetford on this trip. The town of Thetford also includes Post Mills and Union Village. Vermont's tiny villages have been stubbornly reluctant to relinquish their separate identities.

At 6.0 miles, cross the Ompompanoosuc River. That's from an Abnaki word for "at the place of the mushy, quaky land," although it certainly isn't mushy or quaky right here.

About a mile after making a right off Route 113 onto Route 244, start to follow the shoreline of Lake Fairlee. You'll see numerous summer cottages: some rustic ones built in the early part of the century, some modern ones. Traffic will be light, except in July and August when the cottages will be inhabited and the road may be busy. You can cool off at the public access area at 8.3 miles or at the town of Thetford's public beach, called "Treasure Island" (swimming, picnicking, nominal admission fee) at 9.1 miles.

At about 11 miles it will be obvious that you're starting to descend into the Connecticut River Valley. At 12.2 miles, reach the junction with Route 5. Route 5 follows the Connecticut River for much of its length as the Vermont-New Hampshire border. The construction of I–91 has relieved it of most of its heavy traffic, but local traffic can still be significant. Stay right, and exercise caution. From here to East Thetford (5 miles) there will be nearly continuous views of the Connecticut River and the New

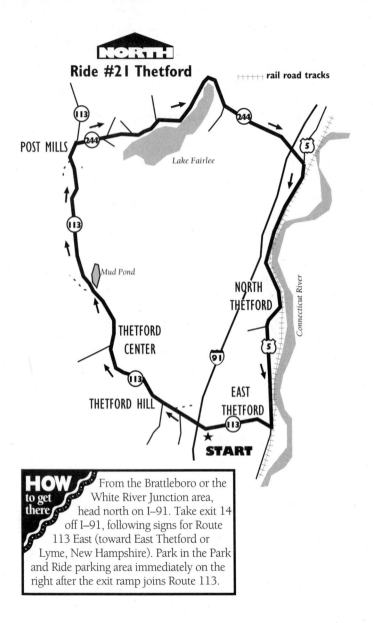

Ride #21 Thetford

NORTH

┼┼┼┼┼ **rail road tracks**

113

244

POST MILLS

Lake Fairlee

244

5

113

Mud Pond

NORTH
THETFORD

Connecticut River

THETFORD
CENTER

113

91

5

EAST
THETFORD

THETFORD HILL

113

★
START

HOW
to get
there

From the Brattleboro or the White River Junction area, head north on I–91. Take exit 14 off I–91, following signs for Route 113 East (toward East Thetford or Lyme, New Hampshire). Park in the Park and Ride parking area immediately on the right after the exit ramp joins Route 113.

DIREC-TIONS at a glance

0.0 Turn left out of Park and Ride area, at exit 14 off I–91, onto Route 113, heading west.

0.9 Village of Thetford Hill. Continue straight on Route 113.

1.1 Thetford Elementary School on left, Thetford post office on right.

2.3 Village of Thetford Center.

2.4 Village Store on right.

2.5 Tucker Hill Road (hard-surface) to left. Continue on Route 113.

3.6 Mud Pond visible on right.

6.0 Village of Post Mills. Bridge over Ompompanoosuc River. Continue on Route 113.

6.2 Baker's General Store on right.

6.4 Make right off Route 113 onto Route 244, following signs for Lake Fairlee.

6.8 Robinson Hill Road (hard-surface) to right. Stay straight on Route 244.

7.4 Begin following shoreline of Lake Fairlee on right.

8.3 Department of Fish and Wildlife Lake Fairlee Access Area on right.

9.1 Treasure Island (Thetford's public beach) on right.

10.2 Hard-surface road to right. Continue straight on Route 244.

11.0 Begin descent to Connecticut River Valley.

11.8 Pass under I–91.

12.1 Junction with Route 5. Turn right onto Route 5 south.

15.1 Village of North Thetford.

16.7 Cemetery on left.

17.1 Village of East Thetford. Make right off Route 5 onto Route 113 west.

18.0 The Lunch Box (sandwiches, and so on) on right.

18.4 Back to Park and Ride area.

Hampshire hills on the other side. Tracks of the Boston and Maine Railroad will be between Route 5 and the river. The river valley has always been a major north-south thoroughfare: Indians and early settlers used the river, the railroad was built in the mid-nineteenth century (copper from just west of here was a major export), and I–91, which parallels Route 5 in the river valley, is now the major north-south artery. Riding along Route 5, you're sometimes in sight of all three: river, railroad, and superhighway.

The cemetery at 16.7 miles is an interesting stop. You're almost to East Thetford now, and this is East Thetford's cemetery. Some of the stones in the back are from the late 1700s, and a few mark the graves of Revolutionary War veterans.

When you reach the turn off Route 5 onto Route 113, prepare to start uphill again. You're parked about halfway between East Thetford and Thetford Hill, and it is indeed uphill the whole way: The good news is that you're doing the easier half of the hill this time.

The Corinths and Goose Green
The Logging Loop

Number of Miles:	12.2
Approximate Pedaling Time:	1½ hours
Terrain:	Moderate hills
Traffic:	Moderate on Route 25, light on rest of trip
Things to See:	Wildlife, Waits River, South Branch Waits River, logging operations
Food:	General stores in East Corinth and South Corinth

This is a beautiful ride in an area of the state that is unfamiliar even to many residents of nearby towns. Road surfaces are good, scenery is rugged, and the general stores are friendly. You may be fortunate enough to catch a glimpse of a moose, bear, deer, or turkey. Except on Route 25, traffic is sparse. However, there is a cautionary note: logging operations in the area require that logging trucks use these roads. You won't encounter many of them, but when you do, it's best to get out of the way. When you see or hear one coming, it's prudent to get off the bike and off the road.

Begin the ride on Route 25, heading northwest and paralleling the Waits River. If you've been riding primarily in the southern part of the state, you'll notice immediately that soil and vegetation are different here. The soil is sandy, and conifers (spruce, fir, and tamaracks) are more prevalent than hardwoods. And this is not the Vermont characterized by bucolic dairy farms. In fact, you're probably more likely to see a moose—or at

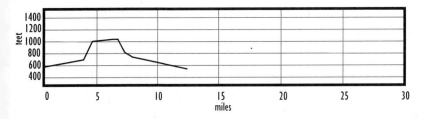

least a deer—than a cow on this trip.

Turn left off Route 25 at 3.2 miles and begin climbing. You'll actually be gaining elevation for the next couple of miles, but the first .2 mile are the steepest.

For the next few miles you'll see ample evidence of the logging industry. Seventy-six percent of Vermont's land is wooded, and that area produces 75 million cubic feet of cut timber annually. It's not surprising that logging, milling, and the manufacture of wood products form a significant portion of the state's economy. Responsibly managed logging operations contribute to the preservation of wildlife habitat and recreational areas and to watershed protection, as well as to the local economy. This ride is an opportunity to look at the timber industry up close.

At 7.1 miles, come to a junction and make a left, following the sign pointing to Goose Green. Cookeville Brook will parallel the road, on your right, for the next half mile. Goose Green is a candidate for smallest place with a name in the state. There's no post office or general store—just a spot where two roads come together and where Cookeville Brook joins Meadow Brook to form the South Branch of the Waits River. Goose Green seems to have one store, which, inexplicably, specializes in lobster trap buoys.

In *Vermont Place Names*, Esther Swift speculates about "Goose Green." Apparently one of the area's early inhabitants raised geese, which were herded to the Boston market in the

NORTH

Ride #22 Goose Green
EAST CORINTH

25

Waits River

25

START
★

25

SOUTH CORINTH

GOOSE GREEN

South Branch Waits River

HOW to get there
From the Brattleboro or White River Junction area, head north on I–91. Take exit 16 off I–91 and proceed west on Route 25 for almost 5 miles to a sizeable gravel parking area on the right. The parking area will be immediately after a blue state highway sign pointing to Slack Farm Maple Products and Crossroads Trading Post. Within sight of the parking area is a road heading south off Route 25, with a bridge over the Waits River.

DIRECTIONS at a glance

0.0 Turn right out of parking area onto Route 25, heading northwest.

0.0 Pass junction with paved road on left. Continue straight on Route 25.

0.3 Route 25 crosses the Waits River (now it will be on your right).

2.2 Village of East Corinth. Hard-surface road to the right. Stay straight on Route 25. East Corinth General Store on right.

3.2 Turn left off Route 25 onto hard-surface road, following signs for Corinth Center and Cookeville.

4.1 Hard-surface road joins from the right. Continue straight.

5.5 Highest elevation.

6.0 Dirt roads join from left and right. Continue straight on hard-surface.

7.1 Junction with another hard-surface road. Go left, following signs for Goose Green.

7.5 Yield sign at hamlet of Goose Green. Road forks. Bear left, following signs for Bradford.

8.5 Dirt road joins from the right. Continue straight on hard surface.

9.2 Village of South Corinth. Crossroads Trading Post on left.

9.6 Dirt road to right. Continue straight on hard surface.

10.5 Saw mill on right.

10.9 Cross bridge over South Branch Waits River.

12.1 Bridge over Waits River and junction with Route 25. Turn right onto Route 25.

12.2 Return to parking area.

poultry equivalent of a cattle drive. Many families' geese were taken south by professional herders, so birds needed to be marked to indicate ownership. The family from this area painted a green stripe on each goose's wing, hence "Goose Green."

From Goose Green to the end of the ride you'll follow the

South Branch of the Waits River. Notice more signs of logging, and, as you approach South Corinth, you'll see more houses and evidence of former farms. There will be numerous spots to cool off in the South Branch, and you'll want to be on the lookout for interesting wildlife in the open meadows along the river.

You'll probably notice the smell of fresh lumber even before you see the sawmill at 10.5 miles. Then it's back to Route 25 and the parking area.

Randolph Center/ Brookfield
Visit the Floating Bridge

Number of Miles: 20.5
Approximate Pedaling Time: 2½ hours
Terrain: Varied, with one long downhill and one significant uphill
Traffic: Light
Things to See: Valley of the Second Branch of the White River, floating bridge in Brookfield
Food: General stores in Randolph Center and East Randolph

This route is a fine pedal, with opportunities for a close-up look at the farms, fields, and villages of central Vermont. Randolph Center and Brookfield are on a ridge. We begin in Randolph Center, descend the eastern side of the ridge, and head north along the valley of the Second Branch of the White River. Then we ascend the ridge again to Brookfield and, finally, head south along the ridge to Randolph Center.

Start the ride on Route 66, heading east out of Randolph Center. This isn't the Route 66 of the old TV series: scenery is great, but cows in the road are probably as close to adventure as you'll get. At 1.3 miles the descent into the valley begins. The sign warning trucks of a steep grade should be a warning to bikers as well. It's a wonderful downhill, but do use your brakes or you'll find yourself exceeding the speed limit. You'll reach East Randolph in short order and make a left onto Route 14 north.

Route 14 is a great Vermont biking road. Although it's a grad-

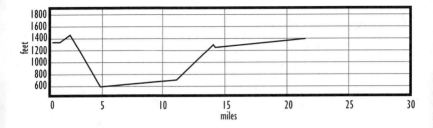

ual uphill (you're following the Second Branch upstream), it
feels quite flat. The valley and hillside farms aren't the manicured weekend retreats seen in some areas of the state. The
smells of manure spreaders in the spring and cornfields in the
summer are smells of the real Vermont.

Turn left off Route 14 onto Route 65 west at 10.8 miles and
start the climb back up the ridge. There had to be a payback for
that magnificent downhill on Route 66, but it's an easier payback than you might expect: the ascent to Brookfield isn't nearly
as steep or as long as the descent from Randolph Center.

It would be unthinkable to pass through Brookfield without
visiting its famous floating bridge, so our route includes a short
side trip. This is thought to be the last bridge of its kind in the
U.S., and you'll probably want a photo. A floating bridge was
first built here in 1884, using oak kegs. The current structure
represents a seventh edition, buoyed up by 374 polyethylene
barrels. Crossing the bridge is an odd sensation. It's quite stable
with just a bike crossing it; but it definitely undulates, like a
raft, as cars pass. The bridge surface isn't more than a few inches
above the surface of the pond. In fact, parts of the bridge become covered with water as cars pass over. **Be careful if you ride
a bike across. The plank surface in the center is wet and very
slippery**. It's safer to ride or walk on the slightly raised walkways
along the side rails.

Route 65 actually continues over the bridge, but our route
backtracks .3 mile to a hard surface right turn off Route 65. The

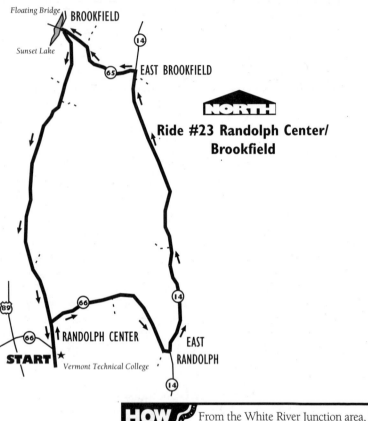

Floating Bridge **BROOKFIELD**

Sunset Lake

14

65 ← **EAST BROOKFIELD**

NORTH

Ride #23 Randolph Center/ Brookfield

89

66

66 ↓ ↑ **RANDOLPH CENTER**

14

START ★ *Vermont Technical College*

EAST RANDOLPH

14

HOW to get there From the White River Junction area, take I–89 north about 30 miles to exit 4. Bear right off the exit ramp, following signs for Route 66 east, Randolph Center, and Vermont Technical College. About 1 mile from the interstate exit, reach a stop sign at a four-way intersection. Go straight across, to the main entrance of Vermont Technical College. Park in one of the nonreserved parking areas immediately ahead.

DIREC-TIONS at a glance

0.0	Turn right out of parking area at Vermont Technical College onto Route 66 east.
0.6	Road forks. Bear right, continuing on Route 66 east.
1.3	Begin descent.
4.3	Village of East Randolph. Turn left at stop sign onto Route 14 north.
7.2	Randolph-Brookfield town line.
10.8	Turn left off Route 14 onto Route 65 west, following signs for floating bridge. Begin uphill.
12.8	Hard-surface road to the left. Continue straight. Road surface turns to dirt.
13.0	Road forks. Bear left to floating bridge.
13.0	Turn around at floating bridge, bear right to retrace route.
13.3	Turn right onto hard-surface road, following signs for Brookfield Center.
19.9	Junction with Route 66. Proceed straight, onto Route 66 west.
20.4	Stop sign in Randolph Center. Proceed straight.
20.5	Make an immediate left to return to parking area at Vermont Technical College.

stretch of road from Brookfield back to Randolph Center is a wonderful rolling biking road: a little hillier than Route 14, but with a good surface, sparse traffic, and clear views to the west.

Waitsfield/Warren
Views of Ski Country

Number of Miles: 14.5
Approximate Pedaling Time: 1½ hours
Terrain: Rolling, reasonably flat on Route 100
Traffic: Light for first half of trip, moderate for second half
Things to See: Covered bridge in Waitsfield, views of Green Mountains, villages of Waitsfield and Warren, Mad River Canoe factory showroom
Food: General stores and restaurants in Waitsfield, general store in Warren

This trip offers a panorama of some of the highest peaks of the Green Mountains and a glimpse of ski country, off season. Waitsfield, our starting point, flourishes largely because of the lure of the Vermont outdoors. You'll see ample evidence of skiing, hiking, canoeing, and biking, and you are likely to encounter kindred spirits along the road or in the shops of Waitsfield and Warren.

Begin at the small parking lot on the west side of Route 100, directly across from the East Warren Road (also called Bridge Street). Cross Route 100 and head east. At .1 mile, cross a covered bridge over the Mad River (the first of many photo opportunities). The Mad River is presumably named for its mad rush of white water in the spring, as snow melts off the mountains.

At .4 mile the road forks. Bear right, continuing on the East Warren Road. It's gradually uphill now for a while, but it's well worth the effort as views of the Green Mountains to the right

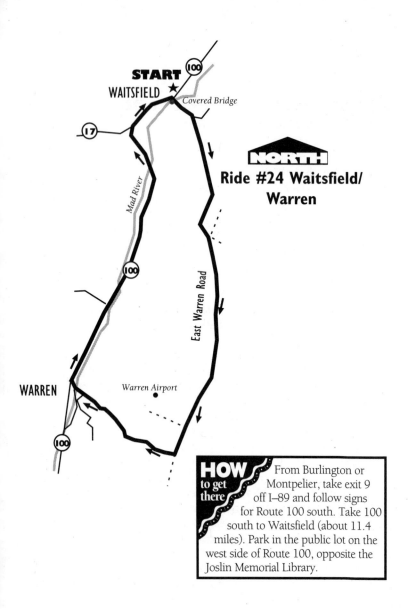

START
WAITSFIELD
100
Covered Bridge

17

Mad River

NORTH

Ride #24 Waitsfield/ Warren

100

East Warren Road

WARREN

Warren Airport

100

HOW to get there From Burlington or Montpelier, take exit 9 off I–89 and follow signs for Route 100 south. Take 100 south to Waitsfield (about 11.4 miles). Park in the public lot on the west side of Route 100, opposite the Joslin Memorial Library.

DIREC-TIONS at a glance

0.0	Parking lot on west side of Route 100. Cross Route 100, proceed east on East Warren Road.
0.1	Pass through covered bridge over the Mad River.
0.4	Road forks. Bear right on East Warren Road.
1.7	Round barn on left.
3.9	Waitsfield-Warren town line.
6.1	Dirt road at right to airport.
6.5	Road forks. Bear right, begin long downhill.
8.4	Stop sign. Bear right.
8.7	Junction with Route 100. Turn right (north) onto Route 100. Traffic will be heavier.
10.4	Cross Mad River.
12.8	Cross Mad River again.
13.5	Route 17 joins Route 100 from the left.
14.0	Business section of Waitsfield.
14.5	Return to parking area.

provide opportunities for some classic Vermont photos. At 1.7 miles, pass a beautifully restored round barn on the left. You can't miss the evidence of three ski areas (Sugarbush, Sugarbush North, and Mad River Glen) on the mountains to your right. At 3.9 miles, note the town line sign at the side of the road. You've left Waitsfield and entered Warren. Along this stretch, several dirt roads will join the East Warren Road. Stay on the hard-surface, continuing south. Some natives, and visitors, too, might debate whether this is the real Vermont. You'll see some very expensive homes, manicured grounds, even the entrance to a polo club. This is a wealthier perspective than we've seen elsewhere in the state.

At 6.1 miles, a right goes to the Warren airport—an interesting side trip to a place that doesn't have much in common with

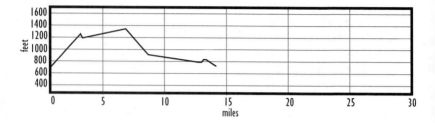

O'Hare. You may have noticed gliders (you won't have heard them) as you were pedaling. This is where they took off. Unless you're taking a side trip to the airport, continue straight. At 6.5 miles, the road forks, and you'll bear right. Test your brakes, as it's downhill now to the stop sign at 8.4 miles.

Our route goes right at the stop sign; but if you're ready for a snack, a left brings you almost immediately to the Warren Store, where baked goods are particularly good. After the right at the stop sign, reach a junction with Route 100 at 8.7 miles. Make a right, and start heading north.

Route 100 is one of Vermont's main roads, and it carries Vermont's version of "a lot of traffic." This particular section of Route 100, between Warren and Waitsfield, is one of just a few stretches that can be recommended for biking. Shoulders are adequate, the road is fairly straight, and visibility is good. Nevertheless, you'll want to concentrate on staying right, returning your attention from the scenery to the road.

You'll be following the Mad River as it flows from Warren to Waitsfield, and there will be several obvious opportunities to stop and get your feet wet. At 10.4 and 12.8 miles you'll cross the Mad River. At 13.5 miles Route 17 joins Route 100 from the left, and you're on the outskirts of Waitsfield again. The business section of Waitsfield has lots of shops and restaurants, and the Mad River Canoe company's factory showroom (look for signs on left) might be a pleasant way to end your visit.

Cabot
The Creamery Tour

Number of Miles: 13.1
Approximate Pedaling Time: 1¾ hours
Terrain: Serious hills
Traffic: Moderate to light
Things to See: Panoramic views, town of Cabot,
Cabot Creamery
Food: General store in Cabot, store at Cabot
Creamery
Facilities: Cabot Creamery

Riders with an aversion to hill climbing may want to skip this one. But those looking for some exercise, magnificent views, and perhaps a stop to watch cheese making at the Cabot Creamery will find this ride a real pleasure.

The first 2.3 miles of the trip are on Route 15. This is an important east-west artery, and it carries a lot of traffic. Exercise caution. The narrow underpass at 0.1 mile warrants extreme caution. The good news is that the first 2.3 miles are all downhill, so the section of the trip with traffic won't take very long.

Be alert for the left turn off Route 15 at 2.3 miles. This will be the first paved left off Route 15. **Get off the bike to make the turn.** (It's a general rule of safety that bikers should get off and assess traffic before making a left turn. In this case it's mandatory. You won't be able to see oncoming traffic as the turn is at the crest of a hill. Get off and listen before you cross.)

After turning off Route 15 you'll start to climb, and you will continue climbing for the next couple of miles. Traffic will seem sparse now. The most common vehicles will probably be whey

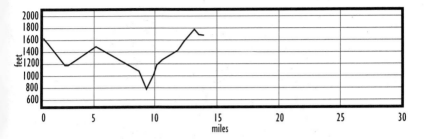

trucks, which look like small tank trucks. You may find yourself getting out of the way of quite a few whey trucks. Whey is a by-product of the cheese-making process, and the Cabot Creamery delivers it to local farms to be used as fertilizer. At about 4.7 miles begin having gorgeous views of the valley ahead. Now it's downhill to Cabot.

Cabot is a typical rural Vermont town, not to be confused with colonial restorations or resort communities in other parts of the state. There's a ballfield, a school, a post office, some buildings that have seen better days, and a general store that stocks just about everything. The Cabot Creamery, .2 mile south of town, is the town's main industry. The creamery is a cooperative, started in 1918 by ninety-four Cabot farmers who pooled their resources in order to produce butter and sell it to the Boston market. The cooperative idea worked and grew. Today Cabot cheeses and other dairy products are sold throughout the Northeast and in specialty stores nationwide. The creamery offers tours, free samples, and a store. A cautionary note: There's a serious uphill ahead. Think twice before buying the five-pound brick of cheddar. (They do mail purchases.)

Our route returns through Cabot, then bears right onto Route 215, heading north. As soon as the road forks, at 8.8 miles, the climb begins. This is a long ascent, but the scenery is magnificent. Be sure to stop and turn around occasionally to look back at the valley. The farms you're passing and those below in the val-

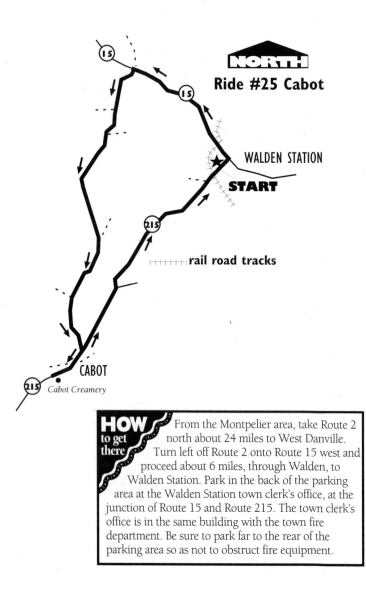

NORTH

Ride #25 Cabot

WALDEN STATION

START

⊢⊢⊢⊢⊢⊢⊢⊢ **rail road tracks**

CABOT

215

Cabot Creamery

HOW to get there
From the Montpelier area, take Route 2 north about 24 miles to West Danville. Turn left off Route 2 onto Route 15 west and proceed about 6 miles, through Walden, to Walden Station. Park in the back of the parking area at the Walden Station town clerk's office, at the junction of Route 15 and Route 215. The town clerk's office is in the same building with the town fire department. Be sure to park far to the rear of the parking area so as not to obstruct fire equipment.

DIREC-TIONS at a glance

0.0 Turn left out of the parking area at the Walden Station town clerk's office onto Route 215. Make an immediate left onto Route 15, heading west.

0.1 Route 15 goes through a narrow underpass. Exercise caution.

2.3 Turn left off Route 15 onto a paved road (not named). This will be the first paved left off Route 15.

4.7 Begin views of valley ahead.

7.7 Stop sign at junction with Route 215. Bear right onto Route 215, heading south.

8.0 Cabot Village Store on right.

8.2 Cabot Creamery visitors center on left. Turn around and retrace route back into village of Cabot.

8.8 Road forks. Bear right, continuing on Route 215 north. Begin climb.

9.9 Road forks. Bear left, continuing on Route 215 north (unmarked).

12.8 Cross railroad track.

13.1 Back to parking area.

ley are probably owned by members of the Cabot cooperative. Again, watch out for the whey trucks. The climb levels off gradually, and at about 12.0 miles, you'll begin the short descent back to Route 15 and the Walden Station town offices.

Lunenburg, VT/ Lancaster, NH
A Connecticut River Tour

Number of Miles:	22.8
Approximate Pedaling Time:	3 hours
Terrain:	Flat
Traffic:	Moderate on Route 2 and through Lancaster. Light for rest of trip.
Things to See:	Views of Connecticut River, Mt. Orne Covered Bridge
Food:	Restaurants, stores, fast food in Lancaster, NH

The Connecticut River is the centerpiece of this two-state ride. There will be almost constant views of the river and of the hills beyond. This is an unusually flat route: an easy pedal with magnificent scenery. Photographers will want to plan this trip for early morning or late afternoon and evening, shooting from the New Hampshire side in the morning and from Vermont in the afternoon. There are no general stores past Lancaster, so bring water and a snack.

The ride starts and ends along Route 2 in Vermont. A major east-west artery, Route 2 is generally not a recommended biking road. In this part of the state, however, it's very flat, has adequate shoulders, and doesn't carry as much traffic as it does farther to the west. Stay right, and stay focused on the road. There will be plenty of time later in the ride to admire the river views.

Cross the river into New Hampshire at 1.5 miles. It's best to get off the bike and use the walkway on the left side of the

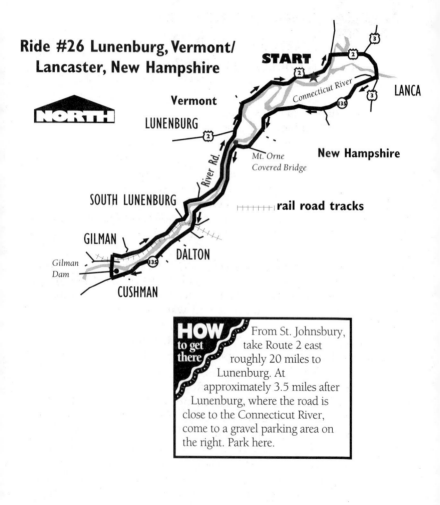

Ride #26 Lunenburg, Vermont/ Lancaster, New Hampshire

NORTH

START

Connecticut River

LANCA

Vermont

LUNENBURG

New Hampshire

Mt. Orne Covered Bridge

River Rd.

SOUTH LUNENBURG

├┼┼┼┼┼┤ **rail road tracks**

GILMAN

Gilman Dam

DALTON

CUSHMAN

HOW to get there From St. Johnsbury, take Route 2 east roughly 20 miles to Lunenburg. At approximately 3.5 miles after Lunenburg, where the road is close to the Connecticut River, come to a gravel parking area on the right. Park here.

0.0 Make right turn out of parking area onto Route 2 and 102, heading north along the Connecticut River.

1.5 Road forks. Bear right on Route 2 and cross bridge over Connecticut River into New Hampshire.

2.5 Road forks. Bear right, continuing on Route 2 east and approaching Lancaster.

3.3 Blinking yellow light. Make right onto Route 135 south.

6.3 River loops very close to road.

8.3 Continue on Route 135 as it makes a sharp left. Mt. Orne Covered Bridge straight ahead.

11.2 Route 142 joins from left. Continue straight on Route 135.

11.2 Railroad bridge over Connecticut River to the right.

11.2 Boat launch on right.

12.4 Town of Dalton.

14.1 Turn right off Route 135, following signs for Gilman, Vermont.

14.5 Cross bridge over Connecticut River and enter Gilman, Vermont. Make an immediate right onto Commercial Avenue, also called River Road.

14.7 Pass Simpson Paper Company plant.

17.9 Junction South Lunenburg Road on left. Continue straight on River Road.

20.0 Mt. Orne Covered Bridge to right.

20.3 Stop sign at junction with Route 2. Make right onto Route 2.

22.8 Return to parking area.

---

bridge. At 3.3 miles, after passing through Lancaster, New Hampshire, bear right onto Route 135 south. Traffic will be scarce now, and scenery will be beautiful. The fertile soil of the Connecticut River Valley makes this area some of New Hampshire's more valuable farm land.

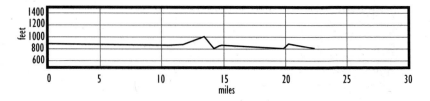

Route 135 makes a sharp left at 8.3 miles. If you go straight, you'll immediately cross the Mt. Orne Covered Bridge into Vermont. If you wish, the trip can be shortened to about 11.3 miles by crossing the Mt. Orne Bridge here and then making a right (see map), cutting the loop about in half. If you wish to do the longer trip, bear left and continue on Route 135 south along the New Hampshire side of the river.

At 14.5 miles, our route crosses back into Vermont. As you cross the bridge, notice the Gilman Dam to the right. As you begin heading north along the Vermont side of the river, you'll pass the Simpson Paper Company, one of the area's largest employers. Logging is an important business in northern Vermont, and some of those logs are turned into paper. Before the days of modern logging rigs and interstate highways, logs were floated down the Connecticut River. Old photos show enormous log jams, with lumberjacks jumping from one floating log to another.

Just north of Gilman, you'll cross the track of the Maine Central railroad. The track will remain between the road and the river for about the next 3 miles. This portion of the trip is idyllic: very gently rolling hills, scarce traffic, and river views that are a photographer's delight. The approach to the Mt. Orne Covered Bridge (at 20.0 miles) is an opportunity for some real calendar photos. This stretch is also a good area for seeing wildlife. Look for ducks, great blue herons, and Canada geese in fall and spring.

At 20.3 miles, come to the junction with Route 2. Views of the river continue to be magnificent, but traffic increases. It's time to focus on the road and pedal defensively. The remaining 2.5 miles of the trip are straight and flat.

Hardwick/Greensboro
A Northern Vermont Sampler

Number of Miles:	23.3
Approximate Pedaling Time:	3 hours
Terrain:	Very steep first 2 miles, then big rolling hills, flat on Route 14
Traffic:	Light to moderate
Things to See:	Towns of Hardwick and Greensboro, Caspian Lake, Willey's Store in Greensboro, village of East Craftsbury, Eligo Pond, wildlife in boggy areas along Route 14
Food:	Restaurants and stores in Hardwick, Willey's Store in Greensboro

This ride takes you through a wonderful variety of Northeast Kingdom scenery; and it's a good workout too. The first couple of miles are a steep climb, but don't let that deter you. Take your time, remembering that getting off and walking for a while is no disgrace.

The route begins in Hardwick, a working-class town with an air of the real Vermont. Unlike some New England towns that boomed with the railroad and now seem on the decline, Hardwick has the feel of a thriving place with lots of energy. The book store across the street from the parking area is an example of a flourishing new business. It has an interesting stock of titles, including a fine collection of works by local Vermont authors. The Northeast Kingdom is home, permanent or seasonal, to a number of well-known literary figures. Locals are pleased with the celebrities in their midst, but they're also proud of the

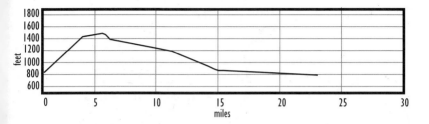

Vermont tradition of protecting *everybody's* privacy. If a Pulitzer Prize winner or a Supreme Court justice is at the next table in the village restaurant, no one is going to mention it.

After climbing out of Hardwick, you'll have the feeling of being on a high plateau with long rolling hills, whose descents almost (but not quite) provide enough momentum for the next ascent.

Greensboro is a quiet village whose population roughly doubles during the summer months. Willey's General Store is a must stop. It embodies the "if we don't have it, you don't need it" philosophy. They have everything. Greensboro's public beach on Caspian Lake (6.6 miles) is a perfect rest or swim stop. As you make a left for the short side trip to the beach, notice the colonial house on the corner. It's a well-preserved example of the "big house, little house, back house, barn" style of architecture found in northern New England, a style of building that was particularly handy in winter.

Several dirt roads join the hard surface after Greensboro. Stay on the asphalt. East Craftsbury is a tiny village. Today it doesn't have a post office or even a general store, but it does have a library. Vermonters cherish a long tradition of dedication to education and free thought, and the tiniest villages have their own libraries.

At 13.5 miles, note the sign warning trucks to use lower gears. Exercise caution, as it's a steep downhill, ending suddenly at a stop sign. If you're going too fast or if the road is wet, stopping could be tricky.

Immediately after making a left at the junction with Route 14, pass Eligo Pond on your left. This is a good example of the

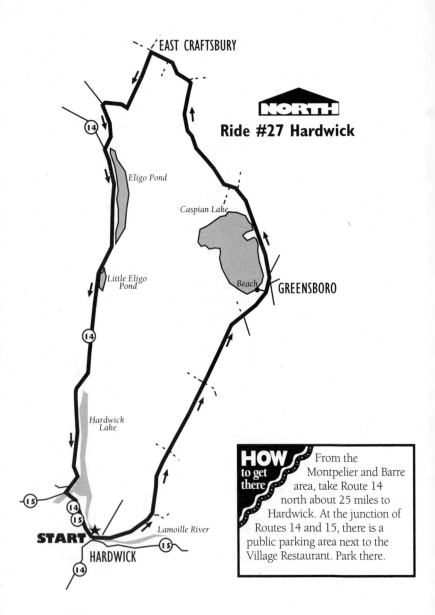

EAST CRAFTSBURY

NORTH

Ride #27 Hardwick

Eligo Pond

Caspian Lake

Little Eligo
Pond

Beach **GREENSBORO**

Hardwick
Lake

HOW to get there From the Montpelier and Barre area, take Route 14 north about 25 miles to Hardwick. At the junction of Routes 14 and 15, there is a public parking area next to the Village Restaurant. Park there.

Lamoille River

START

HARDWICK

DIREC-TIONS at a glance

0.0	Turn left out of public parking area onto Route 15 east (Main Street).
0.0	Make first left off Route 15.
0.1	Cross Lamoille River. Make first right after police station and municipal offices (on right), following sign for Greensboro.
0.3	Road makes sharp left.
0.4	Cross railroad track and start uphill.
2.8	Dirt roads to right and left. Continue straight on hard surface.
4.3	Dirt roads to right and left. Continue straight on hard surface.
5.8	Hard-surface road to right and dirt road to left. Continue straight.
6.2	Begin to see views of Caspian Lake.
6.6	Road to public beach on Caspian Lake on left.
6.7	Intersection in Greensboro. Willey's Store on right. Bear left at intersection.
6.8	Road forks. Bear left, following shoreline of lake.
8.4	Highland Lodge on right.
12.0	Village of East Craftsbury.
12.2	Dirt road to right. Stay on hard surface, which swings left.
13.5	Sign cautioning trucks to use lower gear.
14.0	Stop sign at junction with another hard-surface road. Turn left.
15.0	Stop sign at junction with Route 14. Turn left onto Route 14 south. Eligo Pond on left.
15.9	Eligo Pond public boat access area on left.
17.0	South end Eligo Pond.
17.1	Large sand pit on right.
17.6	Little Eligo Pond on left
21.3	Hardwick Lake on left.
22.0	Hard-surface road to right. Continue straight on Route 14.
22.2	Stop sign at junction with Route 15. Turn left onto Route 15 east, following signs for Hardwick.

22.5 Cross railroad track.
23.0 Use walkway on right.
23.3 Hardwick, public parking area on left.

---

area's many glacial lakes: north-south orientation, long and narrow. The big sand pit on the right at 17.1 miles is another glacial feature—the result of glacial deposition. Note that the soil in this area is sandy. Be careful of soft shoulders, especially if you have skinny tires. After Eligo Pond and Little Eligo Pond, Route 14 follows Alder Brook, which feeds into Hardwick Lake. This stretch of Route 14 is a good wildlife-viewing area. Beaver activity is evident at several spots, waterfowl are common, and salt that washes from the road into the boggy areas is likely to attract deer and moose. You'll probably see footprints in the soil along the roadside.

Reach the junction with Route 15 at 22.2 miles, and prepare for heavier traffic. Starting at about 23.0 miles, there is a walkway on the right side of the road. It's safest to use this, yielding to the occasional pedestrian.

Craftsbury
Uncommonly Beautiful Craftsbury Common

Number of Miles:	11.1
Approximate Pedaling Time:	1½ hours
Terrain:	Moderately steep hills at beginning and end, otherwise rolling
Traffic:	Light
Things to See:	Villages of Craftsbury Common and Craftsbury, panoramic views of Northeast Kingdom
Food:	General stores in Craftsbury

Everyone who is committed to biking in Vermont eventually seems to arrive in Craftsbury—and with good reason. In recent years the Craftsbury area has become a mecca for sports and outdoor enthusiasts. You'll almost certainly encounter other bikers here, and the Craftsbury Sports Centers also attracts paddlers, rowers, hikers, runners, and skiers. Craftsbury has one of the state's most extensive systems of cross-country ski trails, making it a year-round center for outdoor types. The area is un-crowded and unspoiled, and residents seem determined to keep it that way. This short pedal is perfect for an early morning or late afternoon. There aren't a lot of stops; just plan to pedal at a comfortable pace, enjoy the fresh air, and take in the scenery.

The route begins in Craftsbury Common, deemed by many the most picturesque village in the state. It would be tough to dispute that claim. The white colonial homes, church, and school, all around the fenced common, aren't particularly "re-

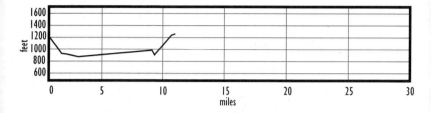

stored," or "preserved." They just haven't changed. Many Vermont towns have a central town green, but few are as large, or as central, as this one. It's easy to imagine it put to its original use, as the common grazing area for livestock. Today there aren't any sheep, but rather baseball, frisbees, picnics, and concerts. A delightful Alfred Hitchock comedy, *The Trouble with Harry*, was filmed in Craftsbury Common. Sterling College, the cluster of buildings on the south end of the common, is a two-year school whose programs emphasize environmental and outdoor studies. The students and the visitors who arrive for outdoor sports seem to have a lot in common.

It's downhill from the village of Craftsbury Common to the village of Craftsbury (at 1.5 miles). With two general stores, a school, and a post office, Craftsbury passes as the business district of the area.

Shortly after making the right onto Route 14, notice the boggy area to the right: a likely area for spotting Northeast Kingdom wildlife, especially in early morning or evening. Between about 6.5 and 7.5 miles, take a look to the right. You can see the village of Craftsbury Common perched on the hill, almost a mile away. Now you're looking at the backs of the houses on the west side of the common.

Watch for the right turn at 8.8 miles. Route 14 can be lovely pedaling. You'll be cruising down a hill at this point, and it would be easy to sail right by the turn. The last couple of miles take you back up the hill to Craftsbury Common. At about 10.5 miles, you'll feel as though you're on a high plateau, with broad views in several directions.

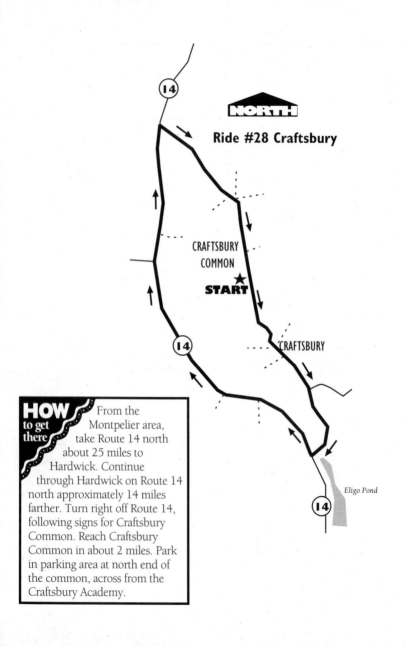

NORTH

Ride #28 Craftsbury

CRAFTSBURY
COMMON
★
START

CRAFTSBURY

14

14

14

Eligo Pond

HOW to get there From the Montpelier area, take Route 14 north about 25 miles to Hardwick. Continue through Hardwick on Route 14 north approximately 14 miles farther. Turn right off Route 14, following signs for Craftsbury Common. Reach Craftsbury Common in about 2 miles. Park in parking area at north end of the common, across from the Craftsbury Academy.

DIREC-TIONS at a glance

0.0	Turn right out of parking area at north end of the green in Craftsbury Common.
0.1	Pass Sterling College.
1.4	Craftsbury Country Store on left.
1.5	Craftsbury General Store and post office on right.
2.1	Hard-surface road to left. Continue straight.
3.2	Junction with Route 14. Turn right onto Route 14, heading north.
3.9	Boggy area to right. Watch for wildlife.
8.8	Turn right off Route 14, following signs for Craftsbury Common.
9.0	Bridge over Black River.
10.3	Dirt road to left. Stay on hard surface road as it swings right.
11.1	Back to parking area on the common.

Unless the weather has been poor (cold rain can have a dampening effect on even the most inspiring scenery), this ride is likely to whet your appetite for more trips in the Northeast Kingdom. The Craftsbury area has miles of dirt roads, which can be fine loops for those with fat tires. Get a map and talk to other cyclists, to people at the general stores, or to the folks at the Craftsbury Sports Center for possibilities.

Barton/Westmore/
West Burke
Lake Willoughby Tour

Number of Miles:	31.6
Approximate Pedaling Time:	4 hours
Terrain:	Moderately steep uphill for first 2.5 miles, descent, then relatively flat
Traffic:	Moderate. Will be more significant during July and August along Lake Willoughby
Things to See:	Lake Willoughby, Crystal Lake, Mt. Pisgah, town of West Burke
Food:	Concession stand at Crystal Lake State Park, general store on Lake Willoughby, general store in West Burke, stores and restaurants in Barton
Facilities:	Crystal Lake State Park

This is the center of Vermont's Northeast Kingdom, an area whose geology and landscape have more in common with northern New Hampshire, Maine, and Quebec than with the rest of Vermont. It feels like a different "kingdom," characterized by conifer forests, deep cold lakes, abundant wildlife, and people whose self-reliance is shaped by a rugged environment. Spring arrives late, fall comes early, and summer is particularly green.

This is a magnificent ride: a little longer than other rides in this collection, but not to be missed. Although it can certainly be pedaled in three hours, it's worth a whole day. Bring a camera, water, and extra clothing. The Northeast Kingdom can be cold, even in summer.

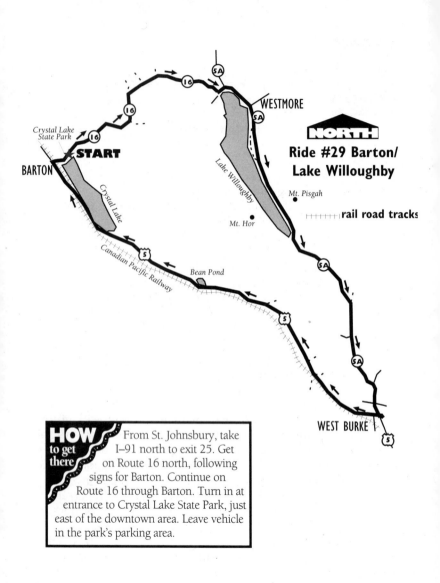

START

Crystal Lake State Park

16

16

16

BARTON

16

5A

WESTMORE

5A

NORTH

Ride #29 Barton/ Lake Willoughby

Lake Willoughby

Mt. Pisgah

++++++ **rail road tracks**

Mt. Hor

Crystal Lake

Canadian Pacific Railway

5

Bean Pond

5

5A

5A

5

WEST BURKE

HOW to get there From St. Johnsbury, take I–91 north to exit 25. Get on Route 16 north, following signs for Barton. Continue on Route 16 through Barton. Turn in at entrance to Crystal Lake State Park, just east of the downtown area. Leave vehicle in the park's parking area.

DIREC-TIONS at a glance

0.0 Turn right out of entrance to Crystal Lake State Park, onto Route 16 heading east.

6.7 Fork in the road. Bear left to arrive immediately at north shore of Lake Willoughby.

6.9 Stop sign at junction with Route 5A. Turn right onto Route 5A south, following signs for Westmore.

7.6 General Store on right.

8.0 Village of Westmore. Hard-surface road to left. Continue on Route 5A.

8.2 Boat launch on right.

9.8 Willoughby State Forest trailhead on left.

10.1–10.4 Waterfalls off rocks on left.

12.1 South end of Lake Willoughby. Boat launch on right.

12.3 Entrance to Cheney House State Park on right.

17.6 Hard-surface road on left. Continue straight on Route 5A.

18.0 Hard-surface road on left. Continue straight on Route 5A.

18.2 Intersection at West Burke. General store on left. Bear right, passing a playground and picnic area on the left.

18.4 Stop sign at a four-way intersection. Bear right (a sharp right) onto Route 5, heading north.

25.3 Bean Pond on right.

28.9 Crystal Lake boat launch on right.

30.1 Bridge over railroad track.

31.5 Intersection with Route 16. Turn right onto Route 16 east.

31.5 Cross railroad track.

31.6 Turn right at entrance to Crystal Lake State Park and return to parking area.

Begin at Crystal Lake State Park—a perfect place to start and end a ride and another reason to plan a whole day for this trip. (A nominal day use fee includes parking, swimming, picnicking.)

The first 2.5 miles, on Route 16 east, are the most difficult part of the trip. Route 16 is a wonderful biking road (good surface, sparse traffic, great scenery), but it's uphill to the top of the watershed between Crystal Lake and Lake Willoughby. Notice the boggy area to your right at about 3 miles. It contains a beaver lodge and is, in general, a good wildlife-spotting area.

More than any other part of Vermont, the Northeast Kingdom reminds us that, geologically speaking, the last ice age wasn't long ago. The bogs, sandpits, and deep narrow lakes are all evidence of the retreat of the most recent continental glacier a mere 11,000 years ago. At 6.3 miles, notice the sandpit to your right (a glacial deposit), and note the holes of bank swallows nesting in it.

At 6.7 miles, you're at the north end of Lake Willoughby. The next 6 miles are going to be memorable. Lake Willoughby is typical of glacial lakes of the area (long and narrow, north to south). Most visitors agree that, although geologically typical, Willoughby is more spectacular than most. It is often compared to the lochs of Scotland. Geologists describing the lake talk about the retreat of the last glacier, a retreat interrupted by a temporary reversal. That was when "fingers" of glacial ice crept back down valleys, carving deep channels and leaving debris at the southern end as they retreated again (hence the uphill climb at the southern end of the lake). Not surprisingly, the cliffs on either side of the lake are mirrored by unusual depths: more than 300 feet at deepest spots. Route 5A hugs the eastern shore of the lake, on what feels like a narrow shelf between the lake and the steep cliffs to the east. The shoulder is adequate, and numerous pull-offs offer opportunities to admire the view. At the southern end of the lake Mt. Hor looms high on the west and Mt. Pisgah rises straight up on the east.

Route 5A south from Lake Willoughby to West Burke is rela-

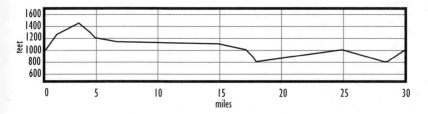

tively flat. It follows the West Branch of the Pasumpsic River, whose boggy banks are habitat for a variety of wildlife. Local papers print regular warnings, especially in spring and fall, about the dangers of hitting moose. They're big, and they're wild animals—keep a safe distance.

The general store in West Burke is a *real* general store, where souvenirs for tourists are just a sideline and life's necessities are the real stock. Directly across from the store is a public picnic area: Buy lunch at the store, and eat it across the street.

Route 5 from West Burke back to Barton is also reasonably flat. It follows the Sutton River (upstream this time) and the Canadian Pacific Railway. The 12 miles between West Burke and Barton provide a snapshot of life in the Northeast Kingdom: logging, hillside farms, winter woodpiles, snowmobiles, camps and trailers, and, finally, Barton's beautiful Crystal Lake. Finish the trip with a swim at the state park, and begin planning another ride in the Northeast Kingdom.

Derby Center/Seymour Lake/Derby Line
Along the Canadian border

Number of Miles:	23.6
Approximate Pedaling Time:	3½ hours
Terrain:	Long rolling hills, some long climbs
Traffic:	Light for most of ride. Moderate along Route 5 between Derby Line and Derby Center.
Things to See:	Town of Derby Center, Seymour Lake, farming regions of Northeast Kingdom, Haskell Library in Derby Line, town of Rock Island, Quebec, town of Derby Line
Food:	Stores in Derby Center, general store in Morgan, general store at Lake Seymour, convenience store and restaurant in Rock Island, Quebec; stores and restaurants in Derby Line
Facilities:	Outdoor facility at Seymour Lake beach

This ride is a sampler of the geographic features of Vermont's Northeast Kingdom. You'll see beautiful lakes, glacial bogs, and conifer forests. And you'll also pass through the high, open dairy farming areas of Orleans County, an area that, strangely, reminds some visitors of the American Midwest. You'll observe a stretch of the world's longest unguarded border and see a demonstration of neighborly, international cooperation alongside the formal system of U.S.-Canadian customs.

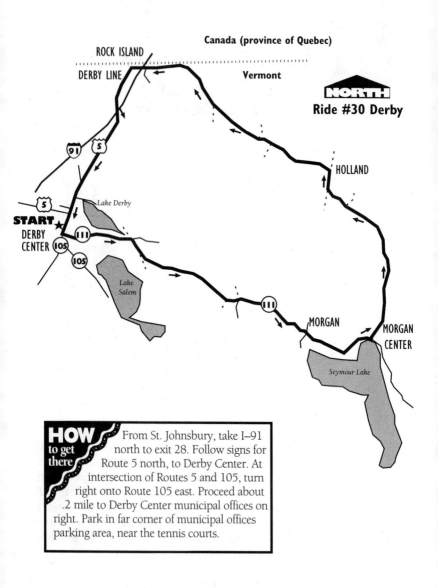

Canada (province of Quebec)

ROCK ISLAND
DERBY LINE

Vermont

NORTH

Ride #30 Derby

91 5

HOLLAND

Lake Derby

5

START
DERBY
CENTER 105 111

105

Lake
Salem

111

MORGAN

MORGAN
CENTER

Seymour Lake

HOW
to get
there

From St. Johnsbury, take I–91 north to exit 28. Follow signs for Route 5 north, to Derby Center. At intersection of Routes 5 and 105, turn right onto Route 105 east. Proceed about .2 mile to Derby Center municipal offices on right. Park in far corner of municipal offices parking area, near the tennis courts.

0.0 Turn right out of Derby Center municipal offices parking area onto Route 105 south.

0.3 Make left onto Route 111 east

1.7 Hard-surface road to right. Continue straight on Route 111.

2.0 Road forks. Bear right, continuing on Route 111 east.

6.3 Potash Kettle on left.

7.1 Town of Morgan. Morgan store and post office on right. Continue straight on Route 111.

8.5 Beginning of town beach on Seymour Lake.

8.9 End of town beach. Turn left off Route 111 onto Valley Road, following sign for Holland.

13.5 Town of Holland.

13.6 Road makes sharp left.

18.9 Cross bridge over I–91. Enter residential area, town of Derby Line.

19.4 Haskell Library on right.

19.5 Stop sign at junction with Main Street (Route 5). Turn left, onto Route 5 south.

19.6 Derby Line park and playground on right.

20.8 Pass under I–91.

23.4 Intersection. Route 5 south goes right. Continue straight, on Route 105 east.

23.6 Back to town offices in Derby Center.

There are conveniently located places to get food on this ride, and there are opportunities for some wonderful stops and side trips. This trip will delight hill-climbing enthusiasts with lots of big rolling hills. When you've finished this ride, you'll proudly want to wear one of the T-shirts that announces "Vermont ain't flat."

The first 8.9 miles, along Route 111 east, contain some good examples of those big hills. Everybody stops, if just for a moment, to rest and to admire the Potash Kettle at 6.3 miles. A sign gives the kettle's history but doesn't explain the significance of potash to colonial settlers. Potash was made by running water through wood ashes, then boiling the remaining solution in a large kettle. It was used in making soap, woolen cloth, linen, and glass and was often the sole cash crop for early settlers.

At about 6.5 miles, begin your final descent on Route 111, to Seymour Lake. The long beach on your right, at 8.5–8.9 miles, is open to the public (free). On a hot day, it may be tempting to stay for a while. The general store on the corner, at 8.9 miles, is a good place to get refueled for the next set of hills, between here and Derby Line.

At 8.9 miles, at the end of the beach on Seymour Lake, be sure to make the left off Route 111, following signs for Holland. This next stretch of road, between Seymour Lake and Derby Line, goes through an important dairy farming region of the state. The land feels very high and open, and you may notice that winds whipping across the open fields from the west can slow you down. Holland isn't much more than a hamlet (no store or post office), but it offers some amazing vistas.

Starting at around 18.0 miles, the views to your immediate right are views of Canada.

At 18.9 miles, as you cross the bridge over I–91, notice Canadian customs to your right and U.S. customs to your left. You're entering the outskirts of Derby Line, Vermont.

Be sure to stop at the Haskell Library, on the right at 19.4 miles. It's half in the United States and half in Canada, and they're very proud of their role as a symbol of international cooperation. A line is painted on the floor, indicating the border, and a chair is placed astride it so you can sit and read in both countries at once.

Our route makes a left at a stop sign at the junction with Main Street (at 19.5 miles), but a quick side trip is recommended. A right turn will take you through customs and into Rock Island, Quebec. People there are certainly friendly, but it's clear right away that the one-hundred-yard pedal has taken you

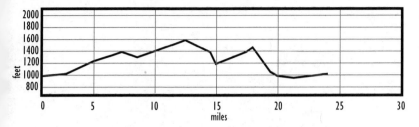

into a foreign country. Customers in the convenience store are chatting in French, and the restaurant across the street has the decided feel of a French cafe (excellent food, but full meals—no sandwiches or snacks).

Most of the rest of the trip, from Derby Line back to Derby Center, is along Route 5 south: More traffic necessitates more caution. And there are just a few remaining (smaller) hills.

Burlington Bike Path
Urban Pedaling at Its Best

Number of Miles: 13.1
Approximate Pedaling Time: 2 hours
Terrain: Flat
Traffic: No vehicles, except on cross streets and at intersections
Things to See: Lake Champlain, city of Burlington, Oakledge Park, Perkins Pier, ferry to New York State, Waterfront Park, North Beach, Leddy Park, Bicycle Path Beach, mouth of Winooski River
Food: Restaurants and vendors along Waterfront Park, concession stands at North Beach and Leddy Park, Charlie's Boathouse near mouth of the Winooski River
Facilities: Oakledge Park, North Beach, Leddy Park

Here's a ride that is triply unique in this collection: It's almost entirely on an official bicycle path, it's an urban ride, and it isn't a loop. It offers incredible views of Lake Champlain and the Adirondacks beyond, and it provides a taste of the kind of recreational and environmental projects that are possible in innovative urban communities. In 1995, *Outside* magazine named Burlington one of seven "dream" cities, citing Burlington's bike path as evidence of a community that's serious about thinking green. A combination of influences, including its small size, the presence of the University of Vermont, and a statewide interest

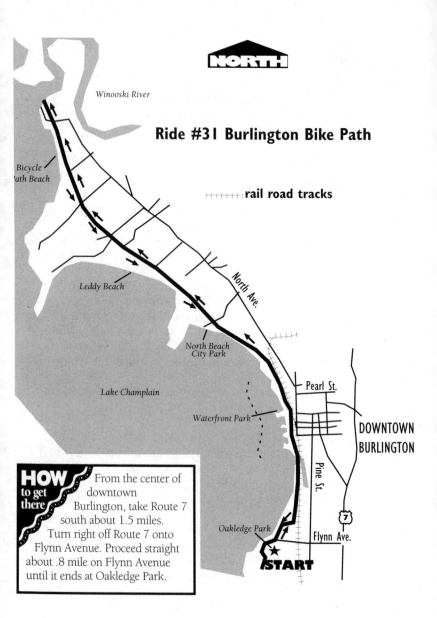

NORTH

Ride #31 Burlington Bike Path

Winooski River

Bicycle Path Beach

++++++ **rail road tracks**

Leddy Beach

North Ave.

North Beach City Park

Lake Champlain

Waterfront Park

Pearl St.

DOWNTOWN BURLINGTON

Pine St.

HOW *to get there* From the center of downtown Burlington, take Route 7 south about 1.5 miles. Turn right off Route 7 onto Flynn Avenue. Proceed straight about .8 mile on Flynn Avenue until it ends at Oakledge Park.

Oakledge Park

7

Flynn Ave.

★ **START**

0.0	Turn right onto bike path near entrance gate in Oakledge Park, heading north toward downtown Burlington.
0.2	Bike path makes right onto Harrison Avenue.
0.4	Harrison Avenue dead ends. Bike path turns left. Railroad track is now to immediate right of the path.
1.2	Railroad yard on right.
1.3	Go through Roundhouse Park.
1.4	Bike path veers right. (Straight to go out on Perkins Pier.)
1.6	King Street Ferry, to New York State, to the left.
1.7	Burlington train station on right.
1.8	Waterfront Park on left
2.3–2.8	Burlington Urban Preserve on left.
3.2	Bike path forks. Continue straight. Bear left for optional stop at North Beach.
4.3	Leddy Park to left.
5.5–5.8	Bicycle Path Beach on left.
6.5	Charlie's Boathouse on left.
6.5	Winooski River straight ahead. Bike Path ends. Turn around and retrace route.
13.1	Return to Oakledge Park.

in environmental protection, make Burlington a friendly place for outdoor types.

The 6-foot-wide asphalt bike path follows the lake front for much of its 7-mile length. It is actually a recreational path, which bikers share with walkers, runners, roller bladers, and baby strollers. It's very flat, has a well-maintained surface, and provides many interesting stops and side trips. The downside of all this is its popularity: It's busy even on cold rainy days. This trip is probably best scheduled for mid-week, perhaps early in the morning. And it will probably take longer than its length suggests. This isn't a ride for speed, and hill climbers will be disappointed. Those looking for a leisurely pedal, splendid views, opportunities for a swim, snacks, and more splendid views will be delighted.

Parking in Burlington can be difficult. Oakledge Park, our starting point, is near the southern end of the bike path, and, at $3.00/car, it's a bargain (picnic areas, beach, bath houses). From Oakledge Park, you begin the ride with a panoramic lakeside view of Burlington to the north.

Pass the King Street Ferry at 1.6 miles. From mid-May to mid-October it makes hourly crossings to Port Kent, New York. Lake Champlain is 107 miles long and 10 miles wide at its widest. The crossing here (its widest section) takes about an hour.

At about 1.7 miles, the main business and shopping area of downtown Burlington is to your right. Church Street, four blocks to the east, has been closed to traffic and is a vibrant pedestrian area lined with shops. It is connected to a downtown underground mall and is considered a model of urban renewal. At 2.3–2.8 miles, pass the Burlington Urban Preserve on your left, between the bike path and the lake. This forty acres of valuable real estate was purchased by the city in 1991 and set aside. It's easy to envision a park or some type of natural area here, and you have to applaud the foresight that claimed this space for preservation. After North Beach, at 3.2 miles, the bike path leaves the lake, and it feels as though you're riding through the woods. It's particularly obvious now that the bike path is following an old railroad bed.

At 5.5 miles, the path rejoins the lake. This may be the most picturesque section of the trip. The shore along here is called Bicycle Path Beach, and you'll notice a couple of lookout areas with wooden steps down to sandy beaches. On a clear day, the Adirondacks are visible on the other side of the lake. On a windy, overcast day, Lake Champlain looks and feels like one of

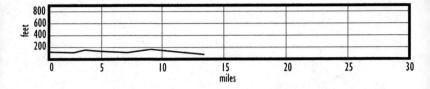

the Great Lakes. There have, in fact, been proposals to designate Lake Champlain the sixth Great Lake.

The bike path ends abruptly at 6.5 miles, at the mouth of the Winooski River. Turn around and retrace the route, making some of the stops you passed by on the way out.

Stowe
By Emily's Bridge

Number of Miles: 11.2
Approximate Pedaling Time: 1½ hours
Terrain: Varied, but not strenuous
Traffic: Light to moderate
Things to See: Stowe recreation path, village of Stowe, views of Green Mountains, Gold Brook, Gold Brook Covered Bridge
Food: Restaurants and stores in Stowe, general store in Moscow
Facilities: Parking area at beginning of bike path

This short ride has it all: Stowe's award winning recreation path, a loop through Moscow, an opportunity for fortune hunters to strike it rich, a haunted covered bridge, and a delightful descent into the village of Stowe. All this, and some exercise too, in less than two hours.

The village of Stowe has thrived on the tourist industry since the nineteenth century, when it was a popular summer resort. Today it's also a center of Vermont's ski industry, and Main Street is crowded with visitors all year long. A majority of Stowe's visitors (and a lot of full-time residents, too) seem to be outdoor types—skiers, hikers, paddlers, and bikers. It isn't surprising that Stowe took a leadership role in establishing a "community created greenway" (its recreation/bike path), which has become a model for similar projects in communities nationwide. Residents of Stowe are proud of their recreation path. They're not only proud of it, they use it—a lot. Don't plan on much speed for the first 3 miles of this trip, as you'll meet or pass all kinds of

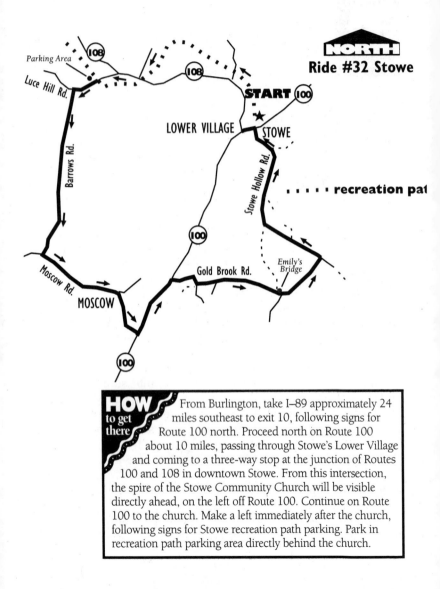

Parking Area

NORTH

Ride #32 Stowe

108

108

108

Luce Hill Rd.

START 100

LOWER VILLAGE

STOWE

Barrows Rd.

Stowe Hollow Rd.

· · · · · **recreation pa**

100

100

Gold Brook Rd.

Emily's Bridge

Moscow Rd.

MOSCOW

100

HOW to get there
From Burlington, take I–89 approximately 24 miles southeast to exit 10, following signs for Route 100 north. Proceed north on Route 100 about 10 miles, passing through Stowe's Lower Village and coming to a three-way stop at the junction of Routes 100 and 108 in downtown Stowe. From this intersection, the spire of the Stowe Community Church will be visible directly ahead, on the left off Route 100. Continue on Route 100 to the church. Make a left immediately after the church, following signs for Stowe recreation path parking. Park in recreation path parking area directly behind the church.

0.0 From parking area behind the Stowe Community Church, head west on the Stowe recreation path.

0.4 Recreation path appears to fork. Bear right on path.

0.7 Cross Weeks Hill Road.

2.4 Cross Route 108. (Get off and walk across.) Continue on recreation path.

2.9 Go through underpass under Luce Hill Road.

3.0 Come out of underpass in parking area. Exit parking area, leaving recreation path and making a right onto Luce Hill Road.

3.3 Turn left off Luce Hill Road onto Barrows Road.

3.7 Pass Stowe High School on left.

5.1 Junction with hard-surface road (Moscow Road). Turn left, following signs for Route 100 and I–89.

6.1 General store in Moscow.

6.1 Road appears to fork. Bear right.

6.2 Cross bridge over Waterbury River.

6.6 Junction with Route 100. Turn left onto Route 100 north.

7.3 Turn right off Route 100 onto Gold Brook Road, start uphill.

7.6 Four-way intersection. Bear left, continuing on Gold Brook Road, with the brook to the immediate left of the road.

8.6 Four-way intersection. Gold Brook Covered Bridge (Emily's Bridge) is to the left. Continue straight on Gold Brook Road.

9.2 Junction with Stowe Hollow Road (paved). Turn left onto Stowe Hollow Road.

10.8 Stop sign. Bear left.

11.1 Junction with Main Street (Route 100). Cross Main Street in front of Stowe Community Church.

folks out having fun (walking, running, strolling babies, as well as pedaling). Plan to relax, enjoying the views, the well-maintained path, and the company.

At 3.0 miles, leave the recreation path and head west on Luce Hill Road. Then watch carefully for the left turn onto Barrows Road. Now you can pick up the pace. Considering its proximity to Vermont's highest peak, this stretch of road is amazingly flat. You'll notice an odd mix of expensive condos and tennis courts next to trailers and houses that have seen better days. This dichotomy often seems to characterize rural Vermont.

Turn left at the junction with another paved road at 5.1 miles. This road has no shoulder, but there isn't much traffic and the speed limit is low. Moscow's general store is coming up at 6.1 miles. It's hard to pass up an opportunity of being able to say you stopped for a soda in Moscow. Then our route makes a left onto Route 100. For the next .7 mile, there will be some real traffic, but the shoulder is wide and visibility is good.

Turn right off Route 100 at 7.3 miles and start uphill on Gold Brook Road. The brook along the side of the road is so named because of the "placer gold" (very tiny nuggets) that have been found here. If you're feeling particularly lucky and have some idea what to look for, you might want to stop and poke around. Finding gold is unlikely, but most people find enough other pretty rocks to make remaining uphills a little more difficult.

Be sure to stop to look at the covered bridge on the left at 8.6 miles. Our route continues straight and does not actually cross the bridge, but most riders will want to make a very short side trip over the bridge, just to see if perhaps it feels a little weird. Although this is officially the Gold Brook Covered Bridge, it is usually referred to as "Emily's Bridge" and is widely thought to

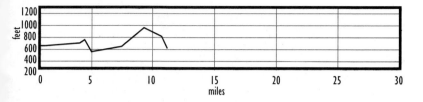

be haunted. No one has been able to confirm who Emily was, or that she lived or died in the area, but there are several variations on the story of Emily's Bridge. The most commonly told recounts how Emily hung herself from a rafter of the bridge after her lover failed to meet her here. In another version she jumped to her death, and in a third she was thrown from her horse on the way to her wedding. In any case, the ghost at Emily's Bridge is reputedly an angry one who slashed at horses in the nineteenth century and at cars as they crossed the bridge in more recent times. In broad daylight it looks like a typical Vermont covered bridge, with a path to a delightful swimming hole on the far side. (Hint for photographers: a little spit on the lens creates a blur on the photo and could serve to enhance the retelling of this ride.)

The remainder of the trip is the return to Stowe—most of it a lovely winding downhill.

Pleasant Valley
A View of Vermont's Highest

Number of Miles:	10.8
Approximate Pedaling Time:	1 hour
Terrain:	Moderate hills
Traffic:	Light, except on Route 15 where will be moderate.
Things to See:	Dramatic views of Mt. Mansfield, Lamoille River, hillside farms of Pleasant Valley
Food:	Stores and restaurants in Jeffersonville, stores in Cambridge

Splendid views of Mt. Mansfield are the the highlight of this trip. The route forms a triangle, of Upper Valley Road, Lower Valley Road, and Route 15. Upper and Lower Valley Roads are nearly ideal for biking (no traffic, good road surface, dramatic mountain views). Route 15 carries too much traffic to be considered ideal, but it parallels the beautiful Lamoille River, and shoulders are adequate.

The trip begins at the Smugglers' Notch Inn in Jeffersonville, whose owners are bicycle friendly. They're avid cyclists themselves, and they like to encourage bicycling as a way of touring the state. They don't mind if cyclists use their parking area—just park at the far end so as not to obstruct regular guests. The inn is named for Smugglers' Notch—the nearby mountain pass between Mt. Mansfield and the Sterling Range of the Green Mountains. Legends recount the exploits of local entrepreneurs who flaunted the embargo on trade with Great Britain (and Canada) during the War of 1812. There is some dispute over the details

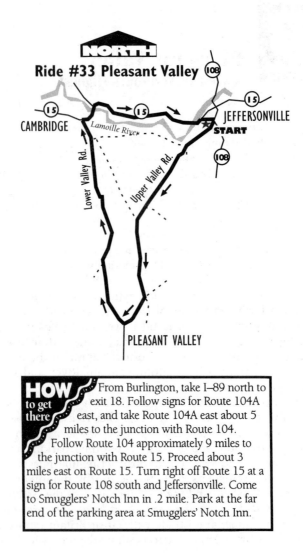

Ride #33 Pleasant Valley

NORTH

108

15

15

JEFFERSONVILLE
START

CAMBRIDGE

Lamoille River

Lower Valley Rd.

Upper Valley Rd.

108

PLEASANT VALLEY

HOW to get there From Burlington, take I–89 north to exit 18. Follow signs for Route 104A east, and take Route 104A east about 5 miles to the junction with Route 104. Follow Route 104 approximately 9 miles to the junction with Route 15. Proceed about 3 miles east on Route 15. Turn right off Route 15 at a sign for Route 108 south and Jeffersonville. Come to Smugglers' Notch Inn in .2 mile. Park at the far end of the parking area at Smugglers' Notch Inn.

DIREC- TIONS
at a glance

0.0	Turn right out of parking area at Smugglers' Notch Inn, onto Route 108 south.
0.0	Make an immediate right onto Upper Valley Road.
2.0	Begin good views of Mt. Mansfield.
3.0	Highest elevation Upper Valley Road.
4.3	Make right turn onto Lower Valley Road.
8.3	Stop sign in Cambridge. Turn right onto Route 15, heading east.
8.6	Cross bridge over Lamoille River and bear right, continuing on Route 15 east.
10.5	Cross bridge over Lamoille River.
10.6	Turn right off Route 15, following signs for Route 108 south and Jeffersonville.
10.8	Return to parking area.

and authenticity of the those legends, but the name has stuck.

Good views of Mt. Mansfield begin at about 2.0 miles. Mansfield is Vermont's highest peak (4,393 feet). Don't worry: Although this trip will have some climbs, they're not up Mansfield. You'll admire its heights from a distance. The mountain is commonly described as resembling the face of a man lying on his back. Landmarks along the summit include the "chin," "nose," "forehead," and "Adam's apple." Local folks consider the view of Mansfield from Pleasant Valley the best—more dramatic than views from other sides. It does loom large, and the closer you get, the more imposing it becomes.

There are a number of side roads (most are dirt) off both Upper and Lower Valley Roads. All are well marked. Unlike some other areas of the state, local towns here have done an admirable job of naming and marking their roads. Just stay on Upper Valley Road until the junction with Lower Valley Road.

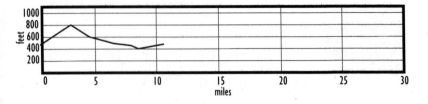

Then make a right. Residents of Pleasant Valley undoubtedly see themselves as a separate community; but there isn't a village—or even a hamlet—that you'll notice. As you travel north again on Lower Valley Road, pause occasionally to look back at Mt. Mansfield. The views from Lower Valley Road are just as impressive as they are from the Upper Valley. The farms along here are what have traditionally been called "hillside farms." Compare these farms with the flat rich fields of the Champlain Basin and the Connecticut River Valley.

When you make a right at the stop sign in Cambridge, you'll be turning onto Route 15. It twists and turns as it follows the Lamoille River. Fortunately, where the turns are the tightest and visibility the poorest, the shoulders are the widest. In just a little more than 2 miles, cross the Lamoille, look for an immediate right to Jeffersonville, and return to the Smugglers' Notch Inn.

Johnson/Jeffersonville/ Waterville
The Lamoille River Loop

Number of Miles: 17.2 miles
Approximate Pedaling Time: 2 hours
Terrain: Gently rolling
Traffic: Moderate on Route 15, light elsewhere
Things to See: Lamoille River, village of Waterville, covered bridge in Waterville
Food: General store in Waterville

This ride begins a couple of miles west of Johnson, a thriving town that makes the best of being a college town in close proximity to big ski country. Johnson feels energetic, but it has escaped the ostentatious demeanor of some ski resort towns. Before or after the ride, visits to the Johnson Woolen Mills and the French Press Cafe are especially recommended. The ride begins at a convenient parking area along Route 15 and follows the Lamoille River Valley west to Jeffersonville. It returns along the north bank of the Lamoille, with a stop in the village of Waterville.

Pedal defensively along Route 15 (first 7.1 miles). Route 15 is a major east-west connection, and it's quite busy. I–89, to the south, has relieved it of some of its heaviest traffic, but Route 15 is still a busy road. Stay right and pay attention. The views of the Lamoille will be even better from the north, so, for now, focus on pedaling and not on views of the river.

After making the right onto Route 108 north (at 7.1 miles), traffic becomes sparse and you can turn your attention to the superb northern Vermont scenery. The Lamoille River will be on your right now, and there will be good views of river, farms, and

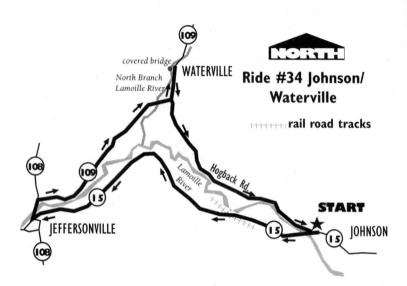

Ride #34 Johnson/ Waterville

┼┼┼┼┼┼┼**rail road tracks**

START

JOHNSON

WATERVILLE

JEFFERSONVILLE

covered bridge

North Branch Lamoille River

Lamoille River

Hogback Rd.

NORTH

HOW to get there From the Montpelier area take I–89 north (west) to exit 10, and get on Route 100 north. Proceed on Route 100 north approximately 20 miles to the intersection with Route 15. Turn left onto Route 15 west, and continue about 6 miles to the town of Johnson. Go through Johnson and proceed about 1.5 miles farther to a gravel parking area on the right, just before a bridge over the Lamoille River. The Long Trail Tavern will be on the left immediately before the parking area.

DIREC-TIONS at a glance

0.0 Turn right out of parking area by bridge over the Lamoille onto Route 15, heading west.

2.0 Cross railroad track.

7.1 Turn right off Route 15 onto Route 108 north.

7.4 Picnic area on right, along the river.

7.5 Turn right off Route 108 onto Route 109.

11.1 Cross bridge over North Branch of the Lamoille River.

11.4 Road forks. Bear left, continuing on Route 109.

11.9 Village of Waterville. Immediately after the general store on the left, turn left off Route 109 onto Church Street.

12.0 Church Street Covered Bridge. Turn around to return to Route 109.

12.1 Turn right off Church Street onto Route 109, heading south again.

12.6 Road forks. Bear left off Route 109 onto Hogback Road.

16.2 Lamoille River is close to road on the right.

17.2 Return to parking area.

Green Mountain peaks in the distance. Mt. Mansfield, Vermont's highest peak, is frequently visible to the south as you pedal along Route 109.

At 11.4 miles, the route makes a short digression from the loop as you bear left toward Waterville, a typical little Vermont community whose general store appears to be the proverbial hub for local news and discussion. A left onto Church Street immediately after the general store takes you to the Church Street Covered Bridge, over the North Branch of the Lamoille. Locals have a favorite swimming hole to the left of the bridge. Bikers may find it convenient to buy a snack at the store and take it to the swimming hole. This is also a good opportunity to admire the bridge, a modest example of a "Queenpost" structure with a span of 60 feet. Most early Vermont covered bridges were built by local farmers and carpenters, who employed essentially the

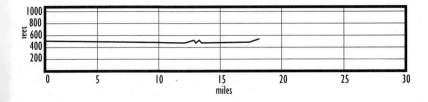

same designs they used in building their houses and barns. Only about a fifth of the state's covered bridges still stand. Fortunately, some small communities like Waterville are preserving these emblems of Yankee craftsmanship and ingenuity.

After a rest stop in Waterville, return to the junction of Route 109 and Hogback Road. Hogback Road is Vermont biking at its best: farms, fields, no traffic, and a gorgeous river. The Lamoille's banks become even more interesting as they change from flat and fertile to steep and rocky. The Lamoille is one of three major rivers that originate in the eastern part of the state and cut directly across the spine of the Green Mountains. (The Winooski and the Missisquoi are the other two.) Geologists explain that these rivers defy what would seem the natural tendency to flow toward the Connecticut River because they are "superimposed" rivers: They are actually older than the Green Mountains. As the mountains rose, the already existing rivers carved through them. Its mix of flatwater and rapids makes the Lamoille a favorite with canoeists and kayakers.

Lake Carmi
Rolling Hills of the North

Number of Miles:	18.3
Approximate Pedaling Time:	2 hours
Terrain:	Long rolling hills
Traffic:	Light (Routes 120 and 236) to moderate (Route 105)
Things to See:	Views of Jay Peak, views of Lake Carmi, village of Franklin, Lake Carmi State Park
Food:	General store in Franklin, Carmi Cafe (seasonal)
Facilities:	Lake Carmi State Park

Vermont's northern farm country is quite unlike any other part of the state. Franklin County is characterized by large prosperous farms, long rolling hills, and enormous panoramic views. On most Vermont bike trips, riders are lucky to be able to see the crest of the next hill. Here, you can often see a mile or more of the route ahead or behind. The hills are long but gradual, and scenery is spectacular. For most of this ride, you're likely to pass as many tractors and other pieces of farm equipment as cars.

The ride begins at a fishermen's pull-off next to the Missisquoi River. The Missisquoi rises east of the Green Mountains, makes a short northward excursion into Canada, then flows westward to Lake Champlain. The Missisquoi is an example of a superimposed river, one that is older than the mountains through which it flows. Hence the apparent illogic of its flowing to Lake Champlain rather than to the Connecticut River.

As you head north on Route 120, there will be impressive

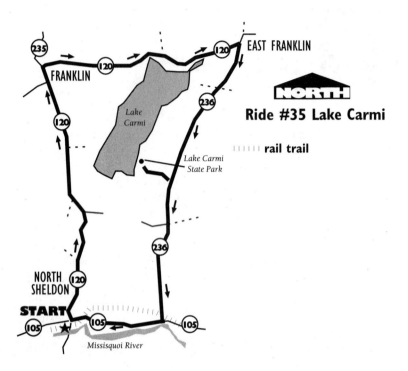

EAST FRANKLIN

235

120

FRANKLIN

120

Lake
Carmi

120

236

NORTH

Ride #35 Lake Carmi

Ⅰ ⅠⅠⅠ Ⅰ **rail trail**

Lake Carmi
State Park

236

NORTH
SHELDON 120

START

105   105   105

Missisquoi River

HOW **to get there** From Burlington, take I–89 north to exit 21 in Swanton. Proceed east on Route 78, through Highgate Center, to the junction with Route 105. Turn left onto Route 105 east.

Continue on Route 105 east about 2 miles to a four-way intersection in North Sheldon. Route 120 is to the left, and an unnamed paved road is to the right. Turn right onto the unnamed paved road and proceed about .1 mile to a gravel pull-off immediately before the bridge over the Missisquoi River. Park here.

DIREC-TIONS at a glance

0.0	Turn left out of parking area next to Missisquoi River, heading back toward Route 105.
0.1	Cross Route 105 and proceed north on Route 120.
2.1	Begin to see views of Lake Carmi ahead.
2.4	Paved road to the right. Continue straight on Route 120.
5.3	Paved road to the left. Continue straight on Route 120.
5.3	Village of Franklin.
5.6	Road forks. Bear right, continuing on Route 120 north.
7.9	Beginning of beach at north end of Lake Carmi.
8.1	Carmi Cafe on left.
9.2	Lake Carmi dam on right.
10.2	Road forks. Turn right off Route 120 onto Route 236 south.
11.0	Four corners, with dirt roads to the right and left. Continue straight on Route 236.
13.2	Entrance to Lake Carmi State Park on right.
14.1	Four corners. Continue straight on Route 236.
16.1	Cross old railroad bed, which is now a snowmobile trail. Optional right turn onto rail trail for riders with heavy-duty mountain bikes. Other riders continue straight.
16.1	Junction with Route 105. Turn right onto Route 105 west.
17.9	Rail trail crosses Route 105. Continue straight on Route 105.
18.2	Turn left off Route 105.
18.3	Return to parking area next to Missisquoi River.

views to the east of Jay Peak(s): Jay Peak, Big Jay, Little Jay, and North Jay Peak. (Better ask a native if you want to sort out which is which.) During any month except June, July, August, and September, they're likely to be snowcapped. At just a little more than 2 miles, begin to see Lake Carmi ahead. Early residents of Franklin County lamented the presence of this "large pond," which took up space where there might otherwise have

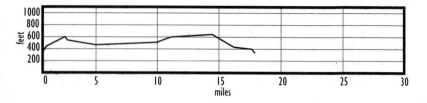

been valuable farm land. Today the farms seem to be happily co-existing with the summer vacationers attracted to the lake.

The general store in Franklin is a good place to stop for a snack, or you might want to take the snack along to the beach at the north end of Lake Carmi, a couple of miles farther on. On a hot day, this is an ideal stop. The beach is immediately adjacent to the road for about .2 mile. It's hard to imagine any biker not stopping for at least a few minutes to admire the lake. It was created by glacial deposition and damming, but unlike most lakes in the northeast part of the state, Lake Carmi has no high cliffs, is fairly shallow, and has a sandy bottom. Naturalists flock to the Lake Carmi Black Spruce–Tamarack Bog to see typical bog vegetation and wildlife. A second opportunity for a swim or a walk along the shore comes at 13.2 miles, as you come to the entrance to the Lake Carmi State Park. The park beach is about 1 mile off Route 236 (minimal admission fee, bath houses).

Views of Lake Carmi continue until about 13.5 miles, when the descent into the Missisquoi Valley begins. If you're on a heavy-duty mountain bike, you may want to make a right off Route 236 at 16.1 miles, onto the old railroad bed which has been turned into a rail trail (of sorts). The trail is covered with large stones, not gravel, and is apparently primarily intended for snowmobile traffic. Only the fattest tires will be able to manage this one. Everybody else will make the right turn onto Route 105 west, just ahead. After the very sparse traffic on Routes 120 and 236, Route 105 feels busy. Stay right and pay attention as you follow the Missisquoi back to the parking area.

Swanton
Flat and Fertile Vermont

Number of Miles:	13.7
Approximate Pedaling Time:	1½ hours
Terrain:	Flat
Traffic:	Light
Things to See:	Town of Swanton, views of Lake Champlain, Swanton Beach, Missisquoi River
Food:	Stores and restaurants in Swanton
Facilities:	Swanton Beach

Only in the Lake Champlain Basin do you find Vermont terrain as flat as this. This is a remarkably easy 13.7 miles, much of it along the lake shore or through flat, fertile farmlands.

Swanton, our starting point, is one of only a few places in Vermont known to be the site of a permanent Indian settlement. The Abnaki village of "Missisasuk" was located here in the early eighteenth century. Excellent fishing and fertile meadows undoubtedly made this an attractive site for the Abnakis, and for the French and English settlers who followed. Today Swanton is still the tribal center for Vermont's nearly 3,000 Abnakis, who continue to seek recognition and rights to land lost to the French and English more than 200 years ago. You'll notice, too, from storefronts, mailboxes, and the phone book that there is a strong French Canadian influence in the Swanton area.

Swanton's town beach, at 1.7 miles, is a a pleasant stop. This section of Lake Champlain is called Maquam Bay ("magquan" means beaver), and that's North Hero Island across the water. Although the beach is rocky, the lake bottom is hard sand, and

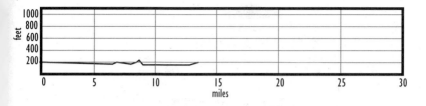

the water remains shallow for a long way out. It's a good spot for a swim. As you look out at the lake, the land you see to the right is called Hog Island, although it isn't an island any more. Sometime in the middle of the nineteenth century a sandbar formed that connected the island to the mainland. Today a large part of Hog Island is the Missisquoi National Wildlife Refuge, a mecca for birdwatchers and naturalists of all sorts.

Route 36 sticks close to the lake shore as it heads south. Typically, there will be houses and cottages to your right, along the beach, and farm fields to the left. Watch carefully for the left turn onto Newton Road at 6.1 miles. Now, as you head east away from the lake, the flat terrain and broad cornfields will almost make you feel as though you're in the American Midwest. At 8.3 miles, a sign lets you know that Newton Road has become Route 38.

At 8.6 miles, notice the Northwest State Correctional Facility off to the right. Immediately after you spot the prison, prepare to turn left off Route 38 onto an unmarked paved road. Still straight and flat, this road takes you by more dairy farms and cornfields. The moderating "lake effect" gives this area an unusually favorable growing season, another reason that Abnaki, French, and English settlers all laid claim to the land.

After the junction and left turn at 12.2 miles the route parallels the Missisquoi River. Although this section of the river is close to the town of Swanton, still be on the lookout for the Missisquoi's famous wildlife. Great blue herons have a large rookery in the wildlife refuge downstream, and herons are a common sight all along the river.

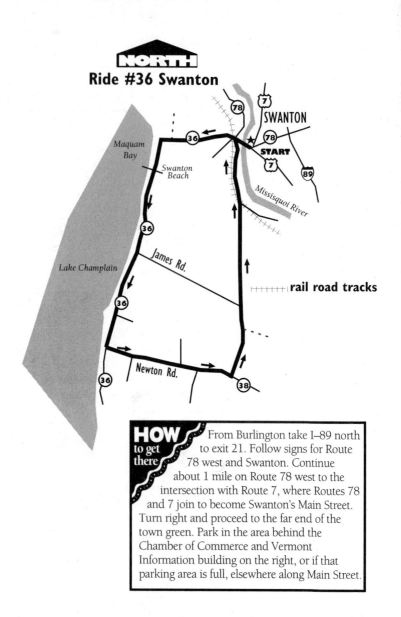

Ride #36 Swanton

NORTH

SWANTON

START

Maquam Bay

Swanton Beach

Missisquoi River

Lake Champlain

James Rd.

┼┼┼┼┼┼ **rail road tracks**

Newton Rd.

HOW to get there   From Burlington take I–89 north to exit 21. Follow signs for Route 78 west and Swanton. Continue about 1 mile on Route 78 west to the intersection with Route 7, where Routes 78 and 7 join to become Swanton's Main Street. Turn right and proceed to the far end of the town green. Park in the area behind the Chamber of Commerce and Vermont Information building on the right, or if that parking area is full, elsewhere along Main Street.

0.0   Turn right out of parking area behind Chamber of Commerce building onto Swanton's Main Street (Route 78).

0.1   Cross bridge over the Missisquoi River.

0.2   Stop sign at a four-way intersection. Turn left onto Route 36.

0.3   Road forks. Bear right, continuing on Route 36.

1.7   Swanton Beach on the right.

4.2   James Road to the left. Continue straight on Route 36.

5.3   Giroux Road to left. Continue straight on Route 36.

6.1   Turn left off Route 36 onto Newton Road.

6.6   Perry Road to the right. Continue straight on Newton Road.

7.6   Middle Road to the left. Continue straight on Newton Road.

8.0   Dunsmore Road to the right. Continue straight on Newton Road.

8.3   Sign STATE HIGHWAY BEGINS. Newton Road becomes Route 38. Continue straight.

8.6   Northwest State Correctional Facility to the right.

8.7   Turn left off Route 38 onto unlabeled hard-surface road.

9.7   Dirt road to the right. Continue straight.

10.1   Hard-surface road to the left. Continue straight.

12.2   Cross railroad track. Junction with another hard-surface road. Turn left.

13.4   Intersection with Route 36 to the left. Continue straight.

13.5   Stop sign. Turn right onto Route 78 east.

13.6   Cross Missisquoi River.

13.7   Back to parking area in Swanton.

Grand Isle
A Grand Ride

Number of Miles: 14.4
Approximate Pedaling Time: 2 hours
Terrain: Flat
Traffic: Moderate on Route 2, light elsewhere
Things to See: Views of Lake Champlain, Hyde Log Cabin, ferry to Plattsburgh, NY, Ed Weed Fish Culture Station
Food: General store in town of Grand Isle, restaurant at ferry landing
Facilities: Grand Isle State Park, Ed Weed Fish Culture Station

The Champlain Islands are ideal for leisurely biking. This route loops around Grand Isle and offers a fine sampling of the island's scenery, history, and industry. There are lots of turns and side roads on this trip, however, so watch directions carefully. There are also several stops and side trips that shouldn't be missed. Although it's a short ride, you may want to plan to spend a whole morning or afternoon.

The ride begins at the Grand Isle State Park. This park is for campers and has no day use areas. However, they graciously make accommodation for biker parking, as long as space is available. Stop at the park office to pay the nominal $1.50/vehicle fee. The park is open mid-May to mid-October. (At other times of the year, bikers may want to begin this ride on the other side of the island, at the ferry landing parking area.) Mileage for

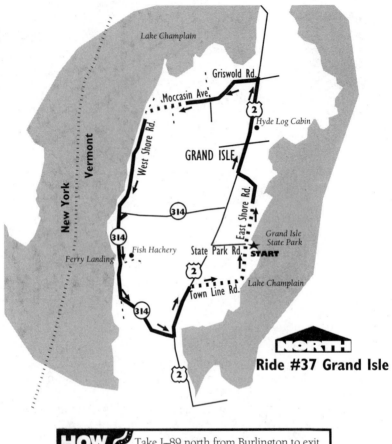

Lake Champlain

Griswold Rd.

Moccasin Ave.

2

Hyde Log Cabin

West Shore Rd.

GRAND ISLE

New York   Vermont

East Shore Rd.

314

314

Fish Hachery

Ferry Landing

State Park Rd.

*Grand Isle
State Park*

★ **START**

2

Town Line Rd.

Lake Champlain

314

2

NORTH

Ride #37 Grand Isle

HOW to get there — Take I–89 north from Burlington to exit 17. Get on Route 2 west, following signs for the Lake Champlain Islands. Continue on Route 2 about 12 miles, past the intersection with Route 314, to a right turn onto State Park Road. Proceed to the end of State Park Road, to Grand Isle State Park. Stop at the office for permission, and to pay a small fee, to park in one of the parking areas.

0.0 Intersection of State Park Road and East Shore Road. Turn right onto East Shore Road (a dirt road), heading north.

0.4 Donaldson Road to the left. Continue straight on East Shore Road.

1.0 Road surface turns to asphalt.

2.0 Junction with Route 2. Turn right onto Route 2, heading north.

2.4 General store on left, in town of Grand Isle.

2.5 Blinking yellow light at a four-way intersection. Continue straight on Route 2 north.

2.9 Hyde Log Cabin on right.

4.0 Four-way intersection. Turn left off Route 2 onto Griswold Road.

5.1 Stop sign at a four-way intersection. Continue straight. Griswold Road becomes Moccasin Avenue.

5.6 Road surface turns to dirt.

5.8 Adams School Road to left. Continue straight.

6.0 Adams Landing Road to right. Continue straight.

6.4 Road surface returns to asphalt. Road swings left and becomes West Shore Road. Adams Landing Road to the right. Continue on West Shore Road.

7.3 Vermont Department of Fish and Wildlife Vantines Access Area to right.

7.6 Quaker Road to left. Continue straight on West Shore Road.

8.5 Allen Road to left. Continue straight on West Shore Road.

8.6 Stop sign at junction with Route 314 (unmarked here). Turn right onto Route 314.

9.5 Blinking yellow light at four-way intersection. Ferry landing to the right. Fish hatchery to the left. Continue straight.

10.3 Route 314 swings left. Dirt road straight ahead. Stay on Route 314.

11.9 Junction with Route 2. Turn left onto Route 2 heading north (sign reads ROUTE 2 WEST).

13.0 Turn right off Route 2 onto Town Line Road (a dirt road).

13.9 Town Line Road makes sharp left and follows lake shore.

14.4 Return to intersection of State Park Road and East Shore Road.

---

the ride begins at the intersection of the State Park Road and East Shore Road.

The first mile of East Shore Road is dirt. Traffic is sparse and views of the lake are fine. At 2.0 miles, East Shore Road joins Route 2, which is the main north-south road joining the islands. There will be traffic, especially during July and August. Our route purposely avoids Route 2 for all but a couple of miles here and another mile near the end of the trip. Pay attention while you're on Route 2 and pedal defensively.

The Hyde Log Cabin is on the right at 2.9 miles. Built in 1783, it is thought to be one of the oldest log cabins in the United States. Today it is owned and maintained by the Vermont Department of Historic Preservation, and it's worth a stop.

Our route crosses the north end of the island, and then heads south along the West Shore Road. At 9.5 miles, come to a four-way intersection, with wonderful little side trips to the right and left. The Lake Champlain ferry to Plattsburgh, New York, is to the right. The ferry is popular with bikers ($4.00 for a round-trip with bike, departures every twenty minutes). The side trip to the left may be even more interesting. It's less than 1 mile to the Ed Weed Fish Culture Station. This is a state-of-the-art fish hatchery, and it's an amazing place to visit. The public is welcome to observe progressive stages in the growth of several varieties of trout and salmon. The self-guided tour goes by the raceways (enormous tanks of running water where juvenile fish are kept), by water treatment plants, by the rushing stream where salmon migrate, and more.

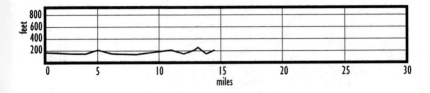

The route continues south following the lake shore, then swings left to cross back to the east side of the island. At 11.9 miles, you're back to Route 2. Then watch carefully for the right turn off Route 2 onto Town Line Road. Town Line Road is a lovely way to end this ride. The road feels as though it's heading straight for the lake, with magnificent views of the Green Mountains in the distance to the east. Then it swings left and parallels the lake shore back to the state park.

Isle La Motte
Another Side of Vermont

Number of Miles:	9.9
Approximate Pedaling Time:	1¼ hour
Terrain:	Flat
Traffic:	Light
Things to See:	St. Anne's Shrine, statue of Samuel de Champlain, views of Lake Champlain
Food:	Cafeteria at St. Anne's Shrine
Facilities:	St. Anne's Shrine

No single image characterizes all of Vermont. Isle La Motte stands as proof of that. Some visitors to Isle La Motte remark on the feeling of having been transported to an Old World religious site. Many note how strong the French Canadian influence is in this part of the state. There's a lot of evidence that this is still Vermont, but Vermont with a slightly different texture.

Our route begins at Saint Anne's Shrine, built on the spot where the first Catholic Mass in Vermont is believed to have been held in 1666. This is also the spot where Samuel de Champlain is thought to have landed in 1609. A statue of Champlain, carved for Montreal's Expo '67, stands on the edge of the island, on the grounds of Saint Anne's Shrine. Isle La Motte boasts a population of 400 regular residents, and tens of thousands of pilgrims and visitors of all faiths who come to Saint Anne's Shrine to seek relief from suffering.

Our ride starts at Saint Anne's Shrine for a couple of reasons: Most bikers will want to visit the shrine at the beginning or end of the ride, and it's a good place to park. There are actually several possible parking areas. The most likely is right along the

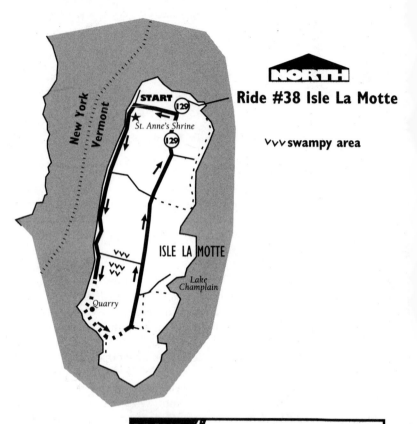

START 129

St. Anne's Shrine

129

ʌʌʌ **swampy area**

ISLE LA MOTTE

New York
Vermont

Lake
Champlain

Quarry

HOW to get there From Burlington, take I–89 north to exit 17. Get on Route 2 west, following signs for the Lake Champlain Islands. Continue on Route 2 northward about 30 miles to South Alburg. In South Alburg, turn off Route 2 onto Route 129 west, crossing the bridge to Isle La Motte. About 1 mile after the bridge, bear right off Route 129, following signs for St. Anne's Shrine. Park in the parking area along the beach, just beyond the shrine.